THE ENGLISH
WAY OF LIFE
A CRITIQUE

Henry C. Ruschmeyer

HENRY CASSELL RUSCHMEYER

ISBN 978-1-0980-4537-1 (paperback)
ISBN 978-1-0980-4538-8 (digital)

Christian Faith Publishing, Inc.
832 Park Avenue
Meadville, PA 16335
www.christianfaithpublishing.com

Printed in the United States of America

To Christopher Powell-Brett, physician on Basil Street, and Neil Lawson-Baker, dentist on Wilton Place, my admirable, private medical practitioners, who helped keep me in good health during my years living and working in London.

*Why is everyone always so shocked when the
truth is spoken, yet remains unmoved by deceit*

From *Blithe Spirit*
by Noel Coward 1942

CONTENTS

PREFACE

The ethic of a people determines how they act in situations demanding right and wrong behavior. It can be said that a people are moral or immoral, even amoral, according to their ethical code. People do make mistakes in spite of an active ethical code. How effective is that code can be seen in the recognition by a people they have done wrong in violation to their ethical code, and the next time they will try to do what is right while making amends for the wrong they have committed. An inoperative ethical code is one in which people never are held accountable for their wrongs, and thus, never make amends for them.

The ethic of a people can be seen through their daily activities by the words they say, and the things they do, publicly and privately. The English are no exception to this means of understanding why a people act the way they do, at home and abroad. The English ethic, if indeed there is one, can be perceived in the printed and spoken word, both activities in which the English excel particularly. It can also be perceived in the way English people conduct themselves, when in their own company or in the company of strangers.

The Bishop of London was heard to say, ironically, to one of his young priests who came to England originally from abroad some years ago, "Haven't you realized by now that this is England where nothing is clear?" The English can be observed to wriggle out of situations in which they feel uncomfortable, many of them being of their own creation. Hence, what they say and do must be carefully recorded and documented, as one's experience suggests, in case Englishmen may deny they ever said or did such and such. However, the English fog may mercifully descend at these awkward moments, and the Englishman may feel quite relieved to sneak away from the inevitable truth, hoping it, too, has disappeared, at least in his lifetime.

Herein, an attempt shall be made to penetrate, fog and all, to try to lay bare the mysteries of the English ethic by one outsider who has lived and worked intimately with the English for seven years, 1989–1996, while regarding some of them as his friends. During this period of time, contact with all strata of English society has been made—from royalty, aristocracy, and upper, middle, and working classes—enabled mainly through a clerical placement in a central London parish, St. Paul's, Knightsbridge, and as a teacher in a private, secondary school in South London, Emanuel, Wandsworth. In all these situations, to fight one's corner against the English bully has been necessary for survival.

London
December 1996

INTRODUCTION

The English often portray themselves as a people who are victims of a cruel world beyond their shores. Such a self-portrait leads them to conclude that all that is evil comes from outside themselves and their island home, including disease, immorality, and strife. The argument then continues, if only *they* would leave us alone, all would be well in England, since we are essentially a people of the best intentions, let alone the best interior qualities enabling us to excel in every way possible above all other people on earth.

The English have succeeded over the centuries in convincing themselves and other people, most notably middle-class Americans in our day, that they are free people, living in a democratic society. English exports to the rest of the world are of a kind that portray only the best the nation has produced, while hiding so much of its evil under cover at home. These exports include Shakespeare, the English Gentleman, the English sense of humor, and a sense of fair play. Unbeknownst to the eager consumer of these goods abroad, these exports are only shared and enjoyed by a small elite back home in England and are solely derived from their privileged world.

Meanwhile, the tottering English economy has been shored up for well over a hundred years, mainly by American money, enabling the country, controlled by a small inward-looking and self-satisfied upper class, to continue to export this superior English image abroad. First, American money provided the means for some very grand English aristocratic families to continue to be grand by marrying rich American heiresses—100 in all—into their impoverished households. Most notable among these arranged marriages was that of the Duke of Marlborough to Consuelo Vanderbilt in the late 1890s. Then the US Lend Lease Act during the Second World War enabled this so-called superior nation to survive under attack from Nazi Germany until America's military might entered the Allied war effort. While, at last, bankrupt after this devastating Second World War, having already been severely shaken by the First (Anglo-German) World War, a generation earlier, with its empire in tatters and the home economy in ruins, millions of dollars, first, as a loan, and then in Marshall Aid money, came pouring into England from Washington to help fix up the English lie and enable the show to go on. Since then American tourist money floods the country each year to enable well-meaning Americans to satisfy their image of "Merrie Olde England" and "the world's oldest democracy"!

Ironically, the majority of the English people have never tasted true freedom, neither do they seem to want it, mostly pretending it does not exist, except as they know it. The conspiracy of ignorance, conceived and perpetrated by the upper class, dating back to the Magna Carta (1215), is in conjunction with the Royal Family, which, in exchange for its lavish lifestyle and prominence, continues over the years to grant favors to the upper class, and more recently, to the entertainment class, most notably in the form of titles and all the prerequisites that go with them. The great majority of the English people, who are lower or working class, docilely assent to their domination by a small elite at the top, while demanding that this elite pays their bills, including housing, food, and medical care. Meanwhile, the small middle class works hard to become upper class. Hence, all the English conspire together against their personal freedom, instead favoring a society that can, hopefully, maximize English prestige and superiority in the eyes of the world. The lower class seems quite content to support this status quo with the dream that one day they will have "a cup of tea with the Queen." This hope may be the highest ambition for most English people; it attests to the brilliance of the English elite in successfully brainwashing the general population for so long, using the arm of the law when necessary, into believing that "Englishness" is the ultimate goal human life can possibly hold up for them. Meanwhile, American money has been used to pay the bills for helping to keep the lower class happy and *in their place*. Alas, it is this ancient charade adopted from the Romans of bread and circuses.

American money, from the American taxpayers, has provided the means to establish the welfare state in England, following the Second World War. The English ruling class has successfully kept this fact secret like so many others, and hidden from sight, until only recently.

The problem with totalitarian societies, such as England's, is that they have so astutely presented themselves to their own people and the rest of the world as something very different from what they really are. Given the facts to the contrary, people are unwilling to face the lie and to make amends for years of oligarchical rule by an elite at the expense of the average Englishman's personal freedom. It is easier, however, to believe the lie than to suffer the embarrassment of being wrong now for centuries. Such an admission would be a terrible blow to English prestige and sense of superiority so the lie would be preferable to many. Only when the English people want to be free will it happen for them. Until then, a conspiracy of silence in all institutions of English life will continue to reign. All will still say that the emperor has new clothes, when in reality, he is stark naked.

This book will attempt to explore England's institutions and life in terms of the prevailing English ethic, engineered and operated on behalf of the ruling class to serve its own interests. In accomplishing this end, these institutions have practiced deceit and denial. Since very little is written down on paper, such as a constitution and bill of rights, England may appear, on the surface, to be an even-handed society, allowing and encouraging eccentrics, as well as bounders, to continue to practice their craft, as long as they do not upset the order of the day. This deceptive English openness allows a wait-and-see policy to prevail, in the event that such individuals on the edge of English life might usefully serve the interests of the Establishment in the end. If these peripheral characters do cause trouble by their activities, the government has the absolute power to clamp down on them immediately, often ruthlessly, as a reading of English history reveals, then and today.

Finally, few courageous individuals speak out against the lie in English life. Instead, most people either emigrate abroad, who cannot stand it any longer, as did the Puritans, en masse in the seventeenth century; or they succumb to it, while attacking foreign cultures and nations as unworthy of English practices and beliefs. England remains a land devoid of high ideals, such as liberty and freedom, and all they imply for the individual. Rather, it is a land of lesser ideals, of countryside and gardens, courtesy and good form, and respect for authority. All of them are really upper-class ideals of an elite who continue to set England's agenda. Any freedom the present-day English people have is granted to them by their "betters" or is derived from riding on the coattails of the American Republic with its clearly enunciated freedoms of speech, religion, press, bearing arms, and assembly, among others. Such an "openness" to these foreign ideals, allowing public utterances in favor of "inalienable rights," points again to the disarming quality of the English upper class in the face of new ways. But in reality, the ruling class will move in, especially when no one is looking, such as the Americans or the European Court of Justice, and crush any challenge to its supremacy, now centuries old.

The result of this self-serving Establishment ethic, with all the hallmarks of expediency, has caused a split in the English national psyche—one which its people find difficult to recognize, let alone, resolve and reconcile. Instead, they remain dependent upon their Masters to show them every step of the way, as long as they refuse to shake them off, claim freedom for themselves, and begin the healing process for their deeply disturbed national, mental health, that often casts a shadow over their own personal sanity as individuals, too. "A house divided against itself cannot stand," Jesus tells his people (Mark 3:25). That house in England is now becoming unstuck, as the country continues to slide economically, and the lie of totalitarianism becomes more evident in a post-Cold War world.

CHAPTER I

Existing Ethical Systems:
Christianity and Utilitarianism

There are two ethical systems that have operated in England over the years, one religious and the other secular. These systems are Christianity and Utilitarianism. Making decisions about right and wrong, and then acting upon them, takes courage on the part of each individual. The Christian ethical system is based upon the teachings of Jesus Christ as found in the Gospels primarily, while Utilitarianism derives from one man originally, Jeremy Bentham (1748– 1832), a London-born philosopher.

It is fair to say that throughout their history as a people, the English have struggled mightily to reconcile their own desires with those of morality. Christianity came late to the Anglo-Saxons, who invaded England successfully in the early AD 500s. These Germanic invaders brought with them a pagan religion, centered upon nature gods, and a social structure based upon the tribe, within which was the military unit of "comitatus." It was a group of warriors bound by their allegiance to their military leader. "The ethical foundations of the comitatus—honour, loyalty, courage—remained the norms of the English and continental warrior aristocracy for centuries thereafter."[1] The resident British,

---

[1] Hollister, C. Warren, *The Making of England 55 BC–1399 AD,* Lexington, Mass 1976, p. 18.

whom the Anglo-Saxons met, were often Celtic Christians, who could claim Alban as their first martyr as early as the third century.

The Germanic invaders brought a rough yet energetic spirit to Britain from which the "ideals of loyalty and honour evolved gradually into the medieval notion of chivalry."[2] Yet they paid a religious price for their robustness as the newly conquered British developed a strong loathing for their conquerors, causing them to flee to western and northern parts of Britain, refusing to share their Christian faith with the barbarians. Hence, a century and a half elapsed between the first conquests and the beginnings of serious missionary work among the Germanic tribes with the coming of St. Augustine in AD 597, sent from Rome by Pope Gregory I to Christianize the Anglo-Saxons.

Previously, the British Christians had shown some misgivings about the demands of Christian ethics when they produced Pelagius, a British priest, who promoted what became known as the Pelagian heresy. Man could achieve salvation by the exercise of his free will rather than divine grace. This emphasis on works appealed to members of the British upper classes, who were keen to emphasize their God-given nature, regardless of the doctrine of original sin taught so fiercely by St. Augustine of Hippo.[3] By supporting Pelagius's teachings, Christians could easily slide away from the Christian ethics of Jesus into practicing quasi-Christian morals, tempered by each passing age, as Jesus's teachings remained an ideal rather than a possibility for any man to achieve. This attempt to squirm out of a particularly difficult ethical situation while still saving face foreshadows the whole of the English ethical dilemma to the present day. It is a misguided and strongly held belief that one can have it both ways and still live with integrity.

This slide away from strict Christian ethical teachings as far back as the late fourth century may have eventually foreshadowed the English secular response to morality with the Utilitarianism of Jeremy Bentham, 1,400 years later. This atheist philosophy believed

---

[2]   Ibid., p. 20.
[3]   Cross, F. L. and Livingstone, B. A. (eds), *Oxford Dictionary of the Christian Church*, London 1974, p. 1058.

that conscience played no part in making an ethical system work. Rather, he decided that the corporal masters of pleasure and pain were sufficient in judging whether a particular human action was right or wrong. Of course, Bentham reasoned man should maximize pleasure and diminish pain. He and his followers, like John Stuart Mill (1806–73), set about exploring the implications of the utilitarian principle for legal and other social institutions, to provide "the greatest good for the greatest number." [4] This mechanistic approach to ethics, using a "hedonic calculus," removed moral decision making forever from the human conscience for all who chose this angst-free approach to morals. Gone were the great religious moral teachings of the ages, such as the Ten Commandments. Bentham and his followers, however, did not take into consideration people who were not of their same background and upbringing, who may have spurned the finer things of life, held dear by an educated, middle class world, and instead, chosen that which might be repellent and painful to some as giving maximum pleasure. Favoring masochism and sadism are examples of an ethical system turned upside down for the Utilitarians.

It is possible to conclude then that the English character, so vastly influenced by its Germanic roots from the Anglo-Saxon invasion of the fourth to the sixth centuries, as well as a Pelagian Christianity of the earlier British inhabitants, continues to struggle with harmonizing a distinctly proud and energetic spirit with a religious ethic that demands humility before God, above all else, and a secular ethic, which tends toward hedonistic, and even, chaotic behavior among individuals in a society that paradoxically favors stability and as little change as possible. Here then is a description of the tension in English ethical life in a people who still believe they can have it both ways—individual self-expression leading to flagrant hedonism alongside social stability and even salvation. Perhaps the English expression *muddle* derives from this apparent ethical conflict.

---

[4] Flew, A. (ed), *A Dictionary of Philosophy*, London 1979, p. 41.

CHAPTER II

Ethics as a Tool of the Establishment: The English Gentleman

The English Gentleman is the creation of the Establishment over the centuries, in attempting to be both Christian and still loyal to the state, and all it stands for amongst the upper classes. The Gentleman is a downsized Christian, who believes in his heart that God is an Englishman, and therefore, England is best. It is difficult to remain patriotic and loyal to one's social class, while at the same time, being a servant of Jesus Christ, who demands complete obedience in love, regardless of race and class. The Gentleman enables some Englishmen to avoid their conscience as Christians, and to live with the assurance all is well with themselves as long as they behave in a prescribed way toward their fellows, always with courtesy and charm, as well as deference to one's betters. Ideally, a Gentleman always fulfils his obligations, is considerate toward women, and exercises personal integrity. The Englishman takes this learned behavior abroad with him, and can always be spotted, or so he hopes, as an English Gentleman.

Originally, only a few Englishmen could afford to travel abroad, beginning with the Grand Tours of the eighteenth century, enjoyed by the sons of aristocrats. Ironically, the English Gentleman abroad is more difficult to recognize today, even though there are thousands of Englishmen annually who make this venture from their island home, "out there." The unwitting foreigners may mistake these new folks for what was traditionally English upper-class behavior and copy what in reality is a more popular version of Englishness as practiced by many people in England today, including body tattoos, rings in noses and ears, and drinking beer out of cans, at home or in public.

In his book entitled *The English Gentleman: The Rise and Fall of an Ideal*, Philip Mason identifies the current problem and exposes a more ancient delusion. "Why did the English establish as a moral code this strange sub-Christian cult of 'behaving like a Gentleman', a word which in other countries acquired no such moral significance? The short answer is that the official religion of England was Christianity and that Christianity demands a standard of conduct altogether too exacting for ordinary mortals if it is taken singly as a moral code. It demands devotion."[5] Such devotion is impossible to achieve when the demands of devotion to the state are so great upon the governing class and the middle class. In hindsight, the Victorians did not enjoy a certainty about beliefs and principles, which their great-grandchildren today, may suppose them to have had. This age, rather, was one of change and turmoil, caused by the Industrial Revolution, discoveries of science and republican revolutions abroad. With religious and social values being challenged by these external forces, the Victorian Englishman grasped at the ideal of the Gentleman as "a code of moral behaviour that was less exacting and involved no commitment to doctrine."[6] The poles of religious and secular life put up by John Henry Newman and the Tractarians on one hand, and Charles Darwin's theory of evolution on the other, was too great a divide and commitment for the upper classes to fathom. The Gentleman provided for them the easy way out, just as for the atheist, Utilitarianism provided another angst-free option. This unwillingness to struggle with right and wrong, the past and the future, says much about the practical and superficial nature of the English mind.

Most un-Christian of all, the code of the Gentleman "was rooted in inequality. It implied differences of rank and fortune in society as well as differences of character and upbringing."[7] People who write

---

[5] Mason, P., *The English Gentleman: The Rise and Fall of an Ideal*, New York, 1982, p. 181.

[6] Ibid., p. 182.

[7] Ibid., p. 226.

about being a Gentleman, such as Philip Mason, see nothing wrong with inequality and elitism. Even in the late twentieth century, this acceptance of class as a fact, grounded upon upbringing and education, is a peculiarly English prejudice, and unfortunate indeed. Part of being an English Gentleman is never admitting you are wrong or seeking forgiveness as the Christian knows it. Humility is not an English attribute as practiced by these upper class Gentlemen. For them, England, of course, is still best.

Another Englishman of the same ilk, and there are and were many of them, is Noel Annan, who writes dreamily about "Our Age,"[8] as if it was the best of times, and without basic fault, only slight imperfections. This was the generation that helped shape post-war Britain. Going back to their beginnings, this small gaggle of middle class and upper class public school, Oxford-Cambridge educated people, were taught to admire as children the ideal of the English Gentleman. This meant that "everyman's first loyalty should be to the country of his birth and the institution in which he served."[9] Ironically, he calls it "the insufferable ideal" and notes that the code of the Gentleman *excludes saints and idealists*. The code rested as noted by P. Mason "on a sense of superiority." Annan believes a failure in this code of the Gentleman to be that they had "no criteria of action other than abiding by the time—honoured practices that were becoming obsolete in their fathers' time."[10] In effect, this older generation had no ideals, Christian or secular, because they disdained such as unworthy of a Gentleman. Yet it was by scraping around the remains of the Gentlemen that "Our Age" came up with its guiding principle, *compassion*, that watered-down Christian virtue once adopted by the English Gentleman. However, the world of Noel Annan was not courageous enough to strike out with new ideals or to abide by Christian teachings in its demands for devotion and humility. In the end, "Our Age" rejected the ideal of the English Gentleman but could find no substitute for it. The muddle in English ethics was not resolved, only

8 Annan, N., *Our Age*, London, 1990.
9 Ibid., p. 26.
10 Ibid., p. 49.

lovingly embraced, by Annan's generation. He seems to believe that because they are Englishmen and the sons of Gentlemen, all will be forgiven. And so that is enough. England is still best. No change is really necessary. The Establishment is still in control of the country. Three cheers!

New leaders, such as John Major, hardly "a Gentleman," by definition, still accept the gentlemanly ideal and perpetrate a system, political and social, that remains elitist and based upon the notion of the superiority of the governing class. The Establishment remains in control of the means of propaganda through education, the legal system, the media, and the Church. Through such institutions, it holds sway upon the English psyche. "Who Cares Who We Are?" reads the editorial title from a recent *Country Life* magazine. Such elitist publications promote the English sense of being best among the nations and indulge its readers in visions of a romantic England set against a cruel, harsh world "out there." The opening sentence is typical in its nostalgia and arrogance: "It used to be said that God must be an Englishman." The upper- and middle-class readers of this sentence really believe this to be true and are flattered by this form of self-indulgence toward them by the writer. One only needs a violin to accompany the rest of the predictable, syrupy drivel that follows: "The icons of the English identity are being pulled down from their altars… The English, not ones to make a fuss, have bent more before the homogenising pressures of Europe, America and corporate multi-nationalism."[11]

Such utterances are commonplace in England daily, whether in the media or private conversation. The Establishment continues to fan the flame of xenophobia among the English by separating them out from the rest of the world as a special people living in a special land. No one and no place on earth compares to it. Just as the Gentleman is uniquely English, so is his country, his values, his beliefs, even his God. No one thing still perpetuates this self-identity as much as the ideal of the Gentleman, that fantastic creation of the Establishment.

---

[11] *Country Life* editorial, "Who Cares Who We Are?", February 1, 1996, editorial page.

John Major may not be one, but he most surely hopes his son or grandson will be one someday. Then everything will be well with the Majors, as it is clearly so with England. It is through this creature, the English Gentleman, the tool of the Establishment, embodying English values and ethics, that the ruling class in England has maintained its power for centuries, by placing him as the Establishment representative in all areas of English life. These include the judiciary, the Parliament, the foreign office, the officers in the military, headmasters of the public schools, principals of Oxbridge colleges, the BBC, the heads of many industries, and the major appointments in the Church of England, including deans and bishops. Such a subtly crafted totalitarian state has few parallels in the history of the world, particularly since its public name is "democracy."

CHAPTER III

Ethics in the Legal System: A Preference for Common, Not Statute, Law

The English have prided themselves, over the centuries, in developing a system of common law, interpreted by judges, which surpasses all other systems of justice on earth. Linked with this common law system is trial by jury and the writ of habeas corpus. Other countries have adopted some aspects of the English legal system, such as the United States of America, while favoring statute over common law, when it conflicts with the Constitution of the United States, or the constitutional laws of a particular state.[12] The ancient common law of England derives its authority solely from past usages and customs or from judgements and decisions of the court, recognizing, affirming, and enforcing such usages and customs. While statute law is found in England too, it is more closely linked with the legislature or Parliament, in which the House of Lords acts as the highest court in the land; whereas, in the United States, a written Constitution and Bill of Rights, as interpreted by a separate, independent Supreme Court, whose judges are appointed for life by the President, takes precedence over any laws enacted by Congress, and hence, subject to being cancelled as unconstitutional. The English legal system lacks

---

[12] Black, H. C., *Black's Law Dictionary* (4ᵗʰ ed), St. Paul's, Minnesota: 1951, pp. 345–6.

such an important check against its activities, which tends to be self-serving for the particular government in power. Thus, Parliament is supreme in the English legal system. Also, it has power through the Crown to appoint judges, who can have the final say in most cases concerning sentencing and appeal. Judges and QCs, or Queen's Counsellors, who can try cases in Crown Court are inevitably figures of the Establishment and, often as not, uphold it since their very jobs have depended upon it.

What troubles the English Establishment so much today are the foreign courts, which once had authority to rule over English cases, particularly the European Court of Justice and the European Court of Human Rights, which are the highest courts of appeal for citizens of the European Union. England, until recently, was a part of the EU and, hence, was subject to its legal decisions. The Establishment's guns came out frequently in the press when the European Court ruled against the English legal system's decisions. Lately, England and Ireland were the only two EU countries that had not incorporated the European Convention on Human Rights into their domestic law or produced a written Bill of Rights.[13]

Since 1985, there have been five significant rulings against England by the European Court of Human Rights. England trails only Italy and Turkey for the number of cases brought over alleged human rights abuses within the thirty-eight-member Council of Europe. Right wing members of the Tory Party use these adverse decisions against English justice as reasons for withdrawing from the European Convention on Human Rights, as well as the EU itself. Writers such as Bruce Anderson of *The Spectator* magazine, a pro-Establishment publication, decry Europe telling England what to do, seeing as previously they were so corrupted by "fascism, dictatorship, and occupation."[14] He goes on to say the latest judgement involving the review of cases of juvenile murderers sentenced to life in prison, "has nothing to do with human rights. Until now the Home

---

[13] "Pressure Grows for Bill of Rights," by Francis Gibb, legal correspondent, *Times*, February 22, 1996, p. 2.

[14] "Britain Must Resist the Court," by Bruce Anderson, *Times*, February 22, 1996, p. 18.

Secretary had the power to prolong detention of juvenile murderers *if he believed* that it was unsafe to release them." This particular kind of English legal blindness stems from an indoctrinated belief that England is best, and thus, *England is always right,* allows one individual to have such awful power over human life that cannot be checked by any apparatus in the English legal system, except by a general election and the possibility of a new government in power. It is all very frightening when one realizes that totalitarian governments in other countries have acted similarly. Typically, the writer of this broadside against the European Court denies the validity of all other legal systems with checks and balances in the free world, including the most obvious one in the United States of America. He says, "But a written constitution is not only inherently anti-democratic, it is a threat to the integrity of the legal process... The malign consequences of this are apparent in the recent history of the United States, where the Supreme Court has become a partisan and unelected legislature." Such sneering and inflammatory words against democratic systems, which obviously work well, are a common method used by the English Establishment throughout English society and in every institution. Half-truths frequently win the day in England for the Establishment. The people reading these words in the *Times* probably know little about the American legal system and are already convinced that England is best. Bruce Anderson wins the day once again for the ruling class. Thus, no change in the English legal system is necessary.

Meanwhile, Parliament can pass whatever draconian laws it chooses, and no one can do a thing about it. From the *International Herald Tribune*, the headline read, "British Pass Broad Search Powers."[15] Allegedly, these powers are aimed at the IRA, but any historian knows that Nazi Germany used such powers to terrorize its people, also under similar pretexts. Now, the police have "unprecedented powers to stop and frisk people on the streets in the interests of fighting terrorism... A person declining to be searched can by

---

[15] "British Pass Broad Search Powers," *International Herald Tribune*, April 4, 1996, p. 1.

arrested, jailed or fined." The writer of the *Herald Tribune* article in this American newspaper, says, "It is one of several laws enacted here in the last two years that have increased powers and curtailed traditional civil liberties in the interests of fighting crime generally." Such utterances frighten Americans while the English people seem to take little notice. This infringement on civil liberties would be used presumably against non-Establishment figures, or anyone from within who may rock the boat and speak out in public against its abuses.

The legal system looks after the upper class as demonstrated in the collapse of Lloyds of London, affecting many Establishment Names. The courts have acted favorably toward them, even though each Lloyd investor initially assumed maximum liability for his or her private investments, amounting to a form of gambling in the insurance market. When Lloyds came up with £8 billion in losses between 1987 and 1992, many Names were hard put to come up with money to cover these losses. A few even committed suicide. The Department of Trade and Industry has acted favorably toward the Names reinsurance company Equitus, to assume all losses arising from policies signed before 1993. Also, a high court judge declared that members of the Rose Thompson Young Syndicate were to "receive damages to restore them to the financial position they would have held if their funds had been handled properly between 1987 and 1989. The judge said the syndicate's underwriter 'fell well below the standards' of a Lloyd's specialist." [16] If the Establishment had not acted favorably toward the 34,000 Names who underwrite the Lloyds insurance market with their personal assets, the Establishment itself would be in danger of collapse. Power then would pass more easily to the people where it surely belongs.

---

[16] "Lloyd's to Raise Its Offer to Names," *International Herald Tribune*, April 11, 1996, p. 3.

CHAPTER IV

Ethics in the Political System: Big Brother Knows Best

English ethics, like so much else that is English, operates from the top down, including the political system, administered by the Establishment and at its whim. To maintain this political system, which is fraught with faults and inequalities, the members of the Establishment, the learned English, fend off criticism in two ways. They either personally attack the individual making the criticism from within the country, or they offensively attack more successful societies and nations outside the Realm, pointing out their failings, which may be no more than a blemish on the face of a beautiful woman. As an example of the first kind of attack, when the Princess of Wales, in a television interview, questioned her ex-husband's suitability to be king, a member of the Parliament, Nicholas Soames, one of Prince Charles' friends, declared in another television interview shortly afterwards that Princess Diana was suffering from "advance paranoia." An example of the second kind of attack is regularly directed at the United States of America and Germany, depending upon the occasion, such as a world sporting event in which England loses or an international crisis, in which English political advice is inadequate or ignored.

The former English Prime Minister, Margaret Thatcher, recently "Stun[ned] Chinese Hosts by Predicting Political Change" in that country, read a headline in the *International Herald Tribune*.[17] The article went on to say that Lady Thatcher also startled many delegates attending the conference of Chinese officials and business leaders by going on "to attack Washington's China policy." In response to this very characteristic English criticism, whether said publicly or privately, a senior Chinese economic official, Wu Jie, said tersely, "Britain had plenty of its own problems, and next time we meet for a conference perhaps we can debate those instead." The last thing in the world the English Establishment wants or would permit is an open debate on the ethics of English life and politics. Then, the whole edifice might come tumbling down, sooner rather than later. By successfully attacking its critics at home, and unwitting challengers abroad, the English political system over the years has avoided looking at its own problems. The end result is that nothing changes, and the inevitable conclusion is that *England is best*. Thus, no real structural problem is dealt with or faced. It is easier to pretend that the country is otherwise sound and happy. When confronted with the horrendous stabbing death of headmaster, Philip Lawrence, in London during 1996, the supporters of the Establishment were heard to say it was "not uncommon," and "we can imagine other situations just like it"!

The process of indoctrination in England, political and otherwise, is subtle and complex, begun at a very early age, especially with members of the Establishment, through their educational system. The renowned English sense of humor, of course, is yet another way of diffusing all arguments and criticism against the English State. One main prop of the Establishment is the BBC, the state-financed television and radio propaganda agency. The weekly broadcast of *Letter from America* by Alistair Cooke on Radio 4 each Sunday morning, at 9:15 a.m. reveals the subtle, ongoing indoctrination process upon which the English Establishment feeds itself and other English people. The enemy object Alistair Cooke (1908–2004) and the Establishment, wish to diffuse and make ridiculous in English eyes,

---

[17] "Thatcher Stuns Chinese Hosts by Predicting Political Change," *The International Herald Tribune*, November 15, 1996, p. 1.

is the United States of America—its political, social, and economic systems—which for 244 years has discredited everything the English Establishment stands for by its very existence. Cooke called America home for years as a newspaper reporter. He resided in great comfort in New York with his family, by now, including children, grandchildren, and even great-grandchildren. He had a lifestyle he would be unable to sustain in England, including digs on Upper Fifth Avenue in New York City and a country house in northern Vermont. Listening to his broadcast over a period of time, which was a regular, de rigueur practice of the Establishment, for young and old alike, he affected the voice of quiet resignation, of a father speaking yet again about somebody else's naughty children. His method was to speak in half-truths, based upon *some* historical knowledge of American history of which his listeners know little or none themselves. He portrayed himself as the wise and patient man whose English listeners hang onto every word he said. The end result of all his weekly blabbering, year after year, was to help keep the Establishment confident that not America but England is the true New Jerusalem. In fact, the English always believed this to be so, but it was good to have "olde Uncle Alistair" assure them of it each week, just in case, they may have some few lingering doubts from time to time. After all, he should know since he *lived* in America.

Cooke's sympathies are those of a New Deal Democrat, an admirer of F. D. Roosevelt, who, of course, came to England's rescue in the 1940s, when it was threatened by Nazi Germany. Roosevelt is England's great American friend, a crony of Winston Churchill's, but not a man always admired in the American Republic because he attempted, sometimes successfully, in usurping important constitutional powers for himself in the name of the Depression and the War. What Cooke and the English Establishment may overlook, however, is that Roosevelt did not support the idea of a British Empire, hence imperialism. Alistair Cooke's January 21, 1996, broadcast attempted to defend a Democrat First Lady, styled after a former one, Eleanor Roosevelt, Hillary Clinton, despite her suspected legal and financial wrongdoings, which are still not resolved. Cooke assured his English listeners that Hillary is the victim of smear campaigns, like her predecessor, Eleanor, because both First Ladies had such high public profiles. He concluded about the Congressional Committee investigating Mrs. Clinton that "though they have been out fishing day after day, and changing the bait, they have not come up with any criminals." By December 1996, we know this statement is not fully true. "Uncle Alistair" ended with a quotation from Mrs. Roosevelt, which he apparently thought applied to Mrs. Clinton, although Eleanor was never a lawyer and never involved in land deals, insolvent savings, and loans banks, and White House sackings, let alone suicides. "You cannot bear grudges, must face defeat, and start new every day."[18]

In his March 3 broadcast, Alistair Cooke was again defending Mrs. Clinton from her critics, saying it is historic for America's first ladies to meddle in politics. He then blasted out at the Republican Party, particularly at "Irish Catholic, in your face, Pat Buchanan." Given England's historic problems with Ireland, this epithet must bring smiles to Cooke's Establishment listeners. He then said that Buchanan's emergence had brought a scary time in US history. And as far as the American people's understanding of their own history, Cooke claimed they hold many misconceptions, regarding first ladies and Pat Buchanans, "due to [their] blank ignorance of American history." Slap one for Pat Buchanan and slap two for the American people. The English Establishment assuredly has reassured itself once again.[19]

By the time of Cooke's March 17 broadcast, the Dunblane Massacre had just occurred, another in a long series of tragedies for the English State and society in recent times. "Uncle Alistair" explained to his eager and, by now, desperately disheartened listeners that "nothing can be done about such incidents as in Scotland. *They always have happened.* Now television has exploded these incidents globally."[20] Cooke suggested then that these events always have happened *all over the world.* We are now just more aware of them. Just to prove his point that everything is still okay in England, Alistair

[18] Alistair Cooke, *Letter from America*, BBC Radio 4, January 21, 1996, 9:15 a.m.
[19] Ibid., March 3, 1996, 9:15 a.m.
[20] Ibid., March 17, 1996, 9:15 a.m.

Cooke offered a barrage of diverting opinions and facts; the same day as Dunblane Massacre, there was a conference on terrorism in the Middle East, and a factory in South Carolina was found to contain nuclear wastes. Besides America has "trigger happy cops," and "America's stumbling blocks are individual rights and liberties," which are "no solution to terrorism." One can only wonder who in London approves Alistair Cooke's "letter" each week from New York City, although the impression his listeners are given is that he just writes down some thoughts on the back of a used envelope an hour or so before each broadcast, and then, lets all his words and thoughts spontaneously flow out. With so calculating and closely run a government as England's, it is difficult to imagine that the powers that be would let someone so influential speak freely without prior consultation with the government as to what the English people *should hear.*

In his April 21, 1996, broadcast, Cooke regaled his listeners with all the acts of terrorism and would-be terrorism in the United States, probably as an assurance to the English that their own country is not unique in this respect. After all, he said, the US president has several death threats every month.[21] On May 5, 1996, Alistair spoke about his contacts over the years with Jack Kennedy, a much-beloved figure in England, but perhaps not universally so in America. Alistair spoke particularly of JFK's rocking chair, which recently was sold for a high price in a New York City auction sale. After all, Cooke said, America's love of myth shows they "buy the *myth* [in the Kennedy rockers] and pretend it was historical fact." Cooke said the word *myth* with particular emphasis, almost dark disgust, as if it were yet another one of those American diseases. He also used Kennedy and Roosevelt as examples of former presidents who had physical ailments, which the press never mentioned, protecting them from embarrassment and public scrutiny. He commented then, "I think it was an admirable profession the press observed. Today it would be an infringement on free speech."[22] Here, Cooke seemed to be reinforcing the English Establishment's objection to the intrusiveness of the press in the lives

---

[21] Ibid., April 21, 1996, 9:15 a.m.
[22] Ibid., May 5, 1996, 9:15 a.m.

of English public figures, particularly inside the ruling class, as well as to having a written Bill of Rights, which included freedom of speech.

So week after week, year after year, "Uncle Alistair" assured the English that they really have been right all along, that their system of government is the best in the world, that the English way of doing things has no equals on earth. He is an example of English hypocrisy, whereby, he benefited daily from the fruits of the world's richest and most powerful nation, safe and secure in his American residences, while subtly attacking the very country that fed him, and all with the blessing of the English Establishment. If he were a courageous and honest man, he would have used his broadcasts to expose the lies of the political system he left behind years ago to live in the American Republic, but then, he would no longer have been on the payroll of the BBC.

A Parliamentary Democracy

England has for at least one hundred years claimed to be a Parliamentary democracy. The idea of Parliament somehow rings in the minds of freedom-loving people, such as the Americans, as synonymous with representative government, similar to the US Congress and the fifty-state legislatures. The English claim to have had a Parliament since the long reign of King Henry III (1216–72). It began as a "talking shop" among the "feudal assemblies of tenants-in-chief sitting with the other members of the king's curia."[23] It carried no idea of election or representation, or of a legislative or tax-voting assembly. It was simply the king's council for debating foreign and domestic politics. This council evolved over the years into the modern notion of a Parliamentary democracy in England, including representational and legislative characteristics. Yet democracy, which means rule by the people, some believe was slow coming to the English political system. In his book entitled *Politics Without Democracy 1815–1914*, Michael Bentley writes that the

---

[23] Trevelyan, G. M., *History of England* (Vol 1), London 1926, first published/and Garden City: Anchor Books edition, 1953, p. 237.

small coterie of individuals who governed in England during this time through Parliament, to which they were theoretically elected, regarded democracy mostly as a "dismal inevitability, or a remote and controllable tendency."[24] He writes that during these years prior to the First World War "all the tendencies of the class structure and its educational arrangements conspired to prevent political leaders from meeting the ordinary people for whose lives they legislated."[25] If then, democracy *does exist* in the English political system today, it is one hundred and five years old, *if that!* Alongside the United States of America, which has had a written and working Constitution and Bill of Rights since 1788, England is a mere fledgling democracy if anything. Rather, absolutist rule has been the time-honored, centuries-old form of the English political system; today, it is still very feudal with the Monarch as head of state. The party in power in Parliament has unchecked authority to act as it wishes on behalf of the Monarch. "If, as some constitutional experts do, one takes the view that 'the Crown in Parliament' is a single entity, then the UK has an 'absolute' government. The question of absolutism...revolves around whether or not there are any powers or constitutional restrictions that can legally prevent a government from taking action. The United States is not absolutist because Congress and the Presidency can check each other (and the Supreme Court), and because the Constitution prohibits certain executive and legislative acts. Britain, however, has no effective Bill of Rights and no separation of powers, and so its government could be described as unlimited and therefore absolutist." This definition and description of an absolutist government, and what it is not, goes on to describe the reasons for it, which turn out to be the English Establishment's reasons for central totalitarian controls. "In practice, the reasons for justifying absolutism tend to be fear of the instability that might be caused by having more than one source of authority, or the use of a justifying theory (theocratic or Marxist, for example) in which rival views cannot be tolerated and some body or group has the absolute right to determine

---

[24] Bentley, M., *Politics Without Democracy 1815–1914*, London, 1984, p. 13.
[25] Ibid., p. 342.

the truth."[26] A keen observer of English life and politics can easily see that the "body or group," which "has the absolute right to determine truth" has been around for centuries; it includes the Crown, the aristocracy, and the upper classes, along with its middle-class supporters, in all no more than 20 percent of the English population, if that! The rest take their marching orders from this group in charge of truth, where "God is an Englishman" and the Monarch is the Supreme Governor of the Church of England.

Representatives of the Establishment, such as Alistair Cooke, make frequent forays by invitation into the world of American churches, universities, and government—anyone from the Archbishop of Canterbury to the prime minster. They take with them the trappings of the English State, which they think will please the Americans, and try to make them think *the English way of life* is rather similar to the American way of life, if not, rather, better!

Anglophiles in America are flattered and cajoled by these visits from the "Mother Country"; whereas, the astute and informed critics of the world scene know that historically, politically, and culturally, England is more of a foreign country to the United States than France or Germany. One such visitor from England, a rather flamboyant and controversial figure in his own country, Robert Boothby, delivered the Radner Lecture at Columbia University in New York City, in late November 1960. One lecture was entitled "The British Parliament" and the other "Politicians in Action." His introductory remarks would set the Anglophiles in the audience all a titter with sighs about English wit, presence, and deference. He began, "How can I follow President Truman's brilliant performance last year with any hope of success? It is an impossible task. Why, then, have I chosen to attempt it? Why have I accepted your most flattering invitation? I will give you an answer in a single word—vanity. It has always been my besetting sin."[27] While admitting that England has no written constitution, he declared that "instead of working to a set of political rules, we have complied with a code of political ethics

---

[26] Robertson, D., *Dictionary of Politics*, London, 1986, pp. 1–2.
[27] Lord Boothby, *My Yesterday, Your Tomorrow*, London, 1962, p. 15.

based on two fundamental principles. These are supremacy of the Common Law, and of the Central Government. The first dates from Saxon times; the second was imposed by William the Conqueror… and continues to this day."[28] The key words in this text are "ethics," "principles," and "supremacy of Central Government." And the key emphasis is that it is old, historical, and traditional. For an American listener, there may be a contradiction here, as how can ethics and principles be part of a strong central government imposed by an absolutist king and still functioning similarly today. Such a notion defies the ethics and principles of the American Republic. So what if this kind of tyranny is historic? Are not they all? In a very typical English Establishmentarian, obfuscation of the truth as it is, Boothby later took common cause with his audience and said, "Absolutism is the eternal enemy. We have, therefore, to reassert our disbelief in human omniscience; to accept the fact of human imperfection; and to deny…the right to inflict…suffering upon humanity in the cause of any creed or dogma."[29] What Boothby would most likely believe is that as long as the English Establishment is in charge of the world, all will be well.

On the other hand, Americans do have a dogma and creed called liberty and freedom for the individual, which is anathema to the English State. Boothby may be giving a subtle rebuke to his American audience not to spread their creed throughout the world, or presume to do so, especially in England, where the Queen and Parliament reigns supreme. Boothby's second lecture, he said was "lollipops," where he described the actions and antics of twentieth-century English politicians, all rather as if it were a light farce. Americans who know that their country is based upon a system of ethics enshrined in the nation's creed cannot be amused by such English capers. "As G K Chesterton [a more thoughtful Englishman] put it: 'America is the only nation in the world that is founded on a creed. That creed is set forth with dogmatic and even theological lucidity in the Declaration of Independence.' The revolutionary ideology which became the

---

[28] Ibid., p. 16.
[29] Ibid., p. 18.

American creed is…distinguished from conservative Toryism, statist communitarianism, mercantilism and noblesse oblige dominant in mechanical state-church-formed cultures," such as England. Thus, "being an American…is an ideological commitment. It is not a matter of birth. Those who reject American values are un-American."[30]

Americans living in England soon discern that most educated English people know little about American history and American political institutions, and what they do know is often inaccurate or distorted through the lens of Englishness. Most horrifying is that they frequently do not know the differences between the United States' three major political documents: the Declaration of Independence, the Constitution, and the Bill of Rights. Painful to the English Establishment's ears is to accept, still, that the United States is the world's richest, most powerful nation *ever*, and that it has the world's oldest written Constitution and functioning democracy.

A Constitution and a Bill of Rights

The English Establishment balks at having to write down a clearly defined statement of how its government is to operate and what rights its people are to have. Rather, a familiar response to queries about such written documents is that the English people have the right to do anything they like until Parliament decides by law that something is forbidden. It is a negative, rather than a positive, statement about liberty and freedom. If Big Brother says no, however, then no it is, and what recourse do the people really have to repeal such offensive laws as might be passed? Really none, except to take to the streets, and that would be un-English!

In late 1995, President Clinton of the United States made a state visit to England and addressed both Houses of Parliament. Writing about the occasion, Matthew Parris of the *Times* said, "The President spoke well. Surrounded by all the ridiculous flim-flam of invented British antiquity, Lord Chancellor in ludicrous fancy dress,

---

[30] Lipset, Seymour Martin, *American Exceptionalism. A Double-Edged Sword*, New York, 1996, p. 31.

the backdrop of unspeakable Victoriana, *Mr Clinton appeared as one from a quieter and deeper-rooted tradition.*" Parris concluded, "I felt ashamed to reflect that the US President was the least vulgar thing in the room. America was restrained, understated: Britain, as ever, pantomime."[31] Indeed, freedom is the most deep-rooted tradition in the history of politics and government, one which remains America's beacon to the world, having embraced it most fully, longer and successfully than any other nation known to mankind. The English Establishment does not like freedom for the English people and disdains publicly, wherever possible, the cause of "republicanism."

Meanwhile, the open debate goes on in England today, whether or not to have a written constitution and a Bill of Rights. Like so much "open debate" in English life, it is designed merely to diffuse the opposition to the Establishment, to create the illusion that the matter has been fully discussed and aired by a free people. However, having a "talk-shop" that has no intention of changing anything at the end of the day is indeed a pantomime of the democratic process. It always stops short of creating something new so the people of England, at last, might feel that it is their country, that there are such people as Mr. and Mrs. England, who are just the same and free as their next-door neighbors.

Each time the constitutional debate surfaces, which seems to raise fears for the continuation of the Monarchy, the Establishment's defenses are regularly trumpeted in the press and broadcasting, decrying any changes and proclaiming the glory of the English system. One favorite, last-ditch, argument for maintaining the system of the Queen in Parliament is that the Royal Family draws important tourist money to the country each year. The assumption is that Americans, Japanese, and others would not frequent those green, misty shores in such numbers if they did not harbor some remote hope of seeing a royal in public. "Monarchists falsely believe the Royal Family somehow retains respect throughout the world, that the world has a fascination for Britain and that being the head of the Commonwealth

---

[31] "Straight Man Steals the Show," by Matthew Parris, *Times*, November 30, 1995, p. 2.

holds a significant advantage for Britain." So says the managing director of Travel and Tourism International Limited who brings more than forty thousand visitors to England each year. Typically, his comments were dismissed by the London Tourist Board, especially with regards to "high-spending Americans."[32] Meanwhile leading Tory MPs, such as John Redwood, argued publicly that the existing "written constitution" works perfectly well. "Britain's settled constitution is *written down* and it does *defend many liberties.* Rather than a new Bill of Rights, we need a self-denying ordinance from national politicians, not to carry on spending and legislating away our freedoms."[33] Mr. Redwood identifies clearly the age-old problem of how to restrain men invested with political power; his solution apparently is that as English Gentlemen, they are capable of monitoring themselves with a little encouragement from the English people.

The Prime Minister, John Major, promised the most thorough-going debate on the future of the British Constitution following Mr. Redwood's remarks above. He then went on to say that at the heart of the English democratic process stands Parliament, whose power and supremacy must not be eroded. He said, "We need no Bill of Rights because we have freedom. Any attempt to define our freedom by statute would diminish Parliament's role as defender of freedoms."[34] Mr. Major is an example of someone on whom, down through the centuries, the subtle genius of the Establishment has operated so effectively. It has recruited him from outside, seduced him with power, position, and the perks of office, including a townhouse and a country estate. Mr. Major surely does not want to upset the applecart of English politics and spoil a good thing for himself and his family. Hence, he speaks in riddles about freedom being possible without clearly defined freedoms. He apparently does not, however, wish to subscribe to Mr. Redwood's fiction that there is a Bill of Rights and a written constitution in England.

---

[32] "Royalty: Still a Draw?" by Marianne Curphey, *Times*, February 2, 1995, p. 22.

[33] "The Crowning Glory," by John Redwood, *Guardian*, June 26, 1996, p. 19.

[34] "Major Pledge to Defend 'Freedoms,'" by Robert Shrimsley, *Daily Telegraph*, June 27, 1996, p. 6.

The threat from abroad is real too, as the Conservative writer William Rees-Mogg frequently points out to his readers. "If the United Kingdom disintegrates, and British democracy is subsumed in a European bureaucracy, the Crown will have lost its function, but the British people will have lost their liberty."[35] Having once fought for independence from this same Crown, so dear to William Rees-Mogg, in the *name* of liberty, American political commentators see through to a clearer vision of personal freedom from their country's own 244-year experience, "free citizens should neither need nor want hereditary or even personalised symbols of unity. Monarchies were junked precisely because people traded their faith in symbols for a confidence that, for better or worse, they could (and ought to) rule themselves."[36] But the English, one is led to believe by their leaders and political commentators, need and value such "symbolic" crutches as the Crown. To the contrary, a recent poll showed that 79 percent of those asked in England favored a written constitution and a Bill of Rights. A constitutional specialist, Professor James Cornford, said, "The British Constitution" really amounts to "what the government of the day thinks it can get away with."[37] This last observation says much about the ethics of the English Establishment, in politics and all other areas of life—that is, doing whatever one can get away with, as long as the Establishment remains in control.

In his book, *The State We're In*, Will Hutton attempts to examine English life and institutions today to try to understand why the country has slipped so far down in the league of nations since the Second World War, both economically and politically. Regarding the English government, he does not mince words as do the politicians and political journalists. "An unwritten constitution organised around the principle that the law is whatever the Monarch assents to in Parliament has no clear democratic rules. Monarchical power has

---

[35] "Crown and Constitution," by William Rees-Mogg, *Times*, August 1, 1996, p. 16.

[36] "Forget the Monarchs and Make Do with Workaday Politicians," by E J Dionne, Jr., *International Herald Tribune*, November 30, 1995, p. 8.

[37] "Constitutional Change in Britain?" by Anthony Lewis, *International Herald Tribune*, October 31, 1995, p. 10.

passed in effect to the majority party in the House of Commons...
There is no formal independence of the judiciary. There is no codified bill of rights. There is no presumption that the activity of
the state should be open and transparent." He concludes that the
Conservative Party in power today "has found itself in charge of a
ruleless state, handed down virtually intact since the settlement of
1688 with universal suffrage bolted on...".[38]

One wonders if anyone in England cares enough to remedy the
situation in favor of individual freedom clearly enunciated and agreed
upon by a constitutional convention and ratified by the people,
rather than to simply talk endlessly about the problem and change
nothing. At year's end, a writer for the *Herald Tribune* commented
on yet another police bill, making its way through Parliament, which
will give the police "broad power to enter anyone's home or office
without a warrant, rummage through papers and plant bugs." The
Tribune writer continued, "Americans fear the power of the state. The
framers of the Constitution wrote in devices to check power, divide
it, defend individuals against it. And the instinctive fear of the centralized state remains as strong today. No such instinct is detectable
in Britain. There is, rather, what must seem to Americans an extraordinary indifference to encroachments of state power on individual
right." In conclusion, the writer believes correctly that the historical difference between the two nations dates back to the American
Revolution, when absolutist rule was turned out of America. He
writes, "Fifty years ago Justice Hugo L. Black replied to an argument
that the US Supreme Court should follow English practice in a particular matter. Those who wrote the American Constitution, he said,
wanted Americans to have far greater protection against official abuse
than the English ever had. The example of the Police Bill makes this
point."[39]

For well over two centuries, the United States has been the
world's classroom for democratic government. The English still

---

[38] Hutton, W., *The State We're In*, London (first published 1988), fully revised
edition, Vintage, 1996, pp. 3–4.
[39] "Startling New Police Bill Meets Yawns in Britain," by Anthony Lewis,
International Herald Tribune, December 31, 1996–January 1, 1997, p. 7.

refuse to join this class and allow individual Englishmen true freedom. The English Establishment works very hard to deny that the English have anything to learn from the Americans, politically and in most other respects.

CHAPTER V

Ethics in the Social Structure: Pretend and Pretense

While the world has changed greatly in the past 244 years, influenced by the industrial, scientific, and technological revolutions, as well as the three great political revolutions in the West—American, French, and Russian—most Western nations have changed accordingly. The post feudal elements that once characterized the European countries have diminished considerably, "although Britain, while also changing, still contains more of these elements than others. In social-structural terms these countries are becoming Americanised."[40] The retardation observed in England regarding social advancement for its people can be most easily explained by the firmly implanted class system to which the English have become accustomed to and secure in for centuries. Their Establishment masters continue to tell them it is the way the world is supposed to be. The class system is in place, furthermore, for the common good. Social class is reinforced in all the institutions of English life to this day, with the educational system assuring that each new generation is properly indoctrinated into their God-given places in society. There is some mobility upwards, depending on the willingness of the individual to adopt and defend the beliefs, manners, attitudes, and speech of the upper-class Establishment.

---

[40] Lipset, p. 289.

In his book *Among the British: An Outsiders View*, the American, Richard Critchfield, originally commissioned by *The Economist* to write a brief sketch on Britain from a foreigner's viewpoint, produced a volume on English life and institutions in the late 1980s, based upon his own observations and many interviews from a wide spectrum of English people. He notes that class is just a fact of life for the English, but never acceptable to the American. "But it is the way the English accept social inequality—their class and cultural divisions—that to many Americans is a personal affront."[41] As Critchfield points out in his book, class has very much to do with accent. Curiously, it was another American, Professor Alan S. C. Ross, in a 1954 essay, who divided the English accent into "U" and "Non-U"—that is, "university speech" and "non-university speech." The rabidly anti-American and upper-class snob Nancy Mitford, of the notorious Mitford sisters, from her place of self-imposed exile outside Paris, popularized this idea so "U" and "Non-U" now meant upper class and non-upper class. So one still hears today in upper class circles only, that so-and-so and such and such is very "Non-U"! or "U," as the case may be. "Accent betrays class, even in the cases of Margaret Thatcher and Edward Heath who have taken elocution lessons; everybody still knows they came from lower-middle class backgrounds."[42] When a member of the Establishment is questioned about such practices, the reply is always a sharp defense. John Ranelagh, once a member of M. Thatcher's staff and born into the upper class himself, rebuffed any criticism that it was wrong for these two previous Conservative Prime Ministers to learn to speak with "such artificial-sounding accents." He said, "Neither would have been Prime Minister if they hadn't. They were paying their dues very publicly." After all, English society welcomes outsiders "provided they made it very clear they want to play the game."[43]

Thus, the right accent as well as school and family have always been the ruling class's way of allowing a few to enter their sacred

---

[41] Critchfield, R., *Among the British: An Outsider's View*, London, 1990, p. 56.

[42] Ibid., p. 57.

[43] Ibid., p. 57.

ranks and to keep all the rest in their place. Other Europeans have taken steps over the years to eliminate this stumbling block at the top to the country's progress, including France, Germany, Italy, and Russia—sometimes, unfortunately, through bloodshed. The English have never mustered the courage to do so, having the tradition of strong central government and oppression longer than the rest. It is difficult to break old habits and to admit one is wrong, especially when it involves a proud people, such as the English. Meanwhile, in modern times, the Establishment has succeeded, up to now, in sugar-coating the Royal Family and all the institutions descending from it as part of "our great English tradition." The cruelty of the English class system is rarely addressed, rather simply accepted as a fact of life, as if the rest of the world lives in such loathsome conditions, too. The insularity of the English people may explain this attitude in part as well as the incredibly subtle, centuries-old indoctrination they have endured without complaining about it or trying to get to the bottom of it. For most of the English, life in their country remains some kind of unfathomable mystery. The English love to speak about and discuss everything that takes their fancy as anyone can see and hear each day, reading the newspapers or watching the television and listening to the radio. Talk, talk, talk always mingled with wry wit and cruel jokes. But there are very few belly laughs, warm cozy cuddles, and tête-à-têtes born out of friendship and cama-raderie, or what the Germans call *Gemütlichkeit*, something Queen Victoria and Prince Albert once tried to foster in frosty England. The class system intrudes so rudely everywhere that everyone has to be on their guard, foreigners and natives alike, unless one is comfort-ably near the top or too old not to be bothered any longer. George Orwell (Eric Blair, 1903–1950), who wrote much about the cruelties of English life in his novels, once tried to describe England in *The Lion and the Unicorn* in 1940. His metaphor for England was a fam-ily, "a rather stuffy Victorian family, with not many black sheep in it but with all its cupboard bursting with skeletons. It has rich relations who have to be kow-towed to and poor relations who are horribly sat upon and there is a deep conspiracy of silence about the source of the family income [i.e., the Empire]. It is a family in which the young are generally thwarted and most of the power is in the hands of irresponsible uncles and bedridden aunts. Still, it is a family. It has its private language and its common memories, and at the approach of an enemy it closes its ranks. A family with the wrong members in control—that, perhaps is as near as one can come to describing England in a phrase." Orwell called his England "the most class-ridden country under the sun...a land of snobbery and privilege, ruled largely by the old and silly."[44]

In reflecting upon George Orwell's remarks on England as a family, one could use the same metaphor about any country on earth. Since all people come from families, one knows too well that some of them are rather nice and some are plain awful. So "family" in itself does not wash away the sins of class consciousness and snobbery. There can be outcasts in some families, while individuals from the beginning have chosen to unhitch themselves from stifling and crippling families for the sake of the individual's well-being—emotional, spiritual, political, and economic. "A deep conspiracy of silence" Orwell identifies in the "English family," at least in economic matters. Such a silence bears down upon the rest of the life, too, as no one wants to ever say that enough is enough, that the Emperor has no clothes. It is easier to remain silent, unless of course one is a Jeremiah whom God will not allow to remain silent, even if it means hardship and persecution for him. Orwell and all the other writers never seem to address why the English people prefer to be silent rather than to change.

As is apparent already, the English Establishment denies whatever unpleasant truth it is accused of being or practicing. Lackeys for the Establishment write columns in newspapers, from the Prime Minister on down, denouncing any criticism which may ring true. These individuals reach beyond England's shores, to castigate the two perceived arch enemies to Englishness—the United States and Germany. One writer, reflecting upon the Victorians love of snobbery, such as found in W. M. Thackerey's *Book of Snobs*, declared that

---

[44] Hennessy, P., *The Lion and the Unicom Repolished*, University of Reading, Department of Politics, Occasional Paper No. 1, February 1990, p. 9.

snobbery no longer exists in England today. And therefore, one may conclude, class consciousness. "Snobbery of such brutish savagery is unknown to most of us these days. Hyacinth Bucket is a character out of the fifties, and we can laugh at her with ease as a bygone absurdity... As a nation we often castigate ourselves as a more class ridden and snobbish society than others, but *there is scant evidence for this.* The Americans' self-image as the classless society is laughable to anyone who has lived there for any length of time. The Barrons and the Vons occupy, if anything, more position of real power in republican Germany than our hereditary peerage."[45] The purpose, of course, for Polly Toynbee writing her particular article was to try to defend the charge by Prime Minister John Major's sister Pat, the widow of a master baker and mother of an operator of color printing machines, that her brother is constantly on guard against slights to his background and social standing by the cliques in a snobbish English world. Polly Toynbee, like any good, loyal Establishment functionary, who writes anti-American and anti-German remarks in the English press daily, must say no to what Pat Dessary, John Major's sister, says is really true. The point, she sadly misses, or knows probably but will not admit it, is that her country suffers not just emotionally and spiritually, but also educationally and economically compared to the United States and Germany, where any class system is more a social gesture among some people rather than an institutionalized characteristic of an entire society. But such is the blindness and hypocrisy of the English Establishment.

In his 1942 play *Blithe Spirit*, Noel Coward has his character Charles speak these lines, "Why is everyone always shocked when the truth is spoken, yet remains unmoved by deceit." Only in England could such a thought arise with such force and clarity, in a country where nothing is meant to be clear. The English weather cannot always be blamed for everything! Well if the weather cannot be blamed this time, then perhaps the old English chestnut "eccentricity" can be used.

---

[45] "The Subtleties of Snobbery" by Polly Toynbee, *Independent*, June 26, 1996, p. 13.

One Englishman wrote for an American audience as follows: "As is well-known, the English are innately, irredeemably, and irreplaceably peculiar. Of all Noel Coward's songs, 'Mad Dogs and Englishmen' is quite rightly the one most generally accepted... But the eccentrics who got written about in earlier days were mostly in civil life and they came from the upper classes... Even so, eccentricity in England is not a class matter. It is a matter of doing what you most want to do and not giving a damn what other people think."[46] Surely so much eccentricity seems to arise in England as a way of survival in a stifling class conscious "family," where so much is criticized that is new and creative, and where much is admired, which is old and static. There are indeed such people as trainspotters, but mostly, the luxury of "doing what you most want to do and not giving a damn about what other people think" is a luxury few in England can afford to practice, except the homeless and the rich. Eccentricity is really then an eruption in a class-bound society, which causes no one, including the eccentric, any problems or disturbances, while maintaining the hegemony of the ruling class in England.

One memorable English eccentric from the aristocracy was Stephen Tennant whose family's wealth depended mostly on the lower classes continuing to drink Tennant's beer. Philip Hoare writes of this profligate twentieth-century figure who spent most of his life at parties, travelling, visiting friends, and drawing pictures. Writing of Stephen in later life, his friend Cecil Beaton, photographer of the aristocracy, from lower-middle class origins, noted that Stephen's brain was "'still a remarkable instrument—and he shows himself to be a real and true eccentric with deep passion for the things he loves, living in a hovel of his own making with a frenzy and zeal' that made Cecil feel his own existence was 'quite humdrum.'"[47] English social ethics allows such people to continue undisturbed, squandering money and time in comparatively useless pursuits, as if England had all the time in the world to do what it liked with no one to whom to account for it—not its own people, not other nations, not the

---

[46] "Portrait of the British" by John Russell, *New York Times*, March 9, 1986.

[47] Hoare, P., *Serious Pleasures, The Life of Stephen Tennant*, London, 1990, p. 344.

future, not God. The arrogance of the English class system over the centuries has come to inform its own Establishment that "England is time," and therefore, there is no need to advance, to improve, to expand, so that others in the society might benefit, too. Rather, it is a system designed for the elite, to serve the elite at its pleasure, albeit their "serious pleasures." Meanwhile, the rest of the world is passing England by.

CHAPTER VI

Ethics in Education: A Class Unto Itself

Most social historians identify the perpetration of social class in the structure of the English educational system, much to the Establishment's chagrin and horror, and continual denial. Living in England over a number of years, and mingling with the middle and upper classes who send their children to private, fee-paying schools—which the English euphemistically call "public schools"—one soon develops a sense that Eton and a few other select schools within their ethereal orbit of English education are the key to understanding how the Establishment successfully continues to keep its stranglehold on English politics, culture, and life. Only 10 percent of the English school-age population go to private schools, which numbers upwards a thousand institutions. So many of England's leaders within the Establishment have then gone the next step to Oxford and Cambridge for the final process of indoctrination into "Englishness." Statistics published in August 1996 show that nearly half of Oxford's intake is from the privileged 10 percent of the fee-paying schools. The other places are filled with able, state school applicants who come from the other 90 percent of the school-age population.[48] Even though some of these students come from the one hundred-odd grammar schools in the country, the historic link

---

[48] "Public Schools Win More Places at Oxford" by John O'Leary, *Times*, August 26, 1996, p. 1; "Entering Oxford" Editorial, *Times*, August 26, 1996, p. 7.

between the public-school and grammar-school boys still operates smoothly, with the latter emulating and admiring the former whenever possible and throughout their lives. They can be observed to work in tandem with one another, where the grammar-school boys back up the public-school toffs. Noel Annan records, "The manners of Our Age were public school manners; and it was easier to be accepted if you adopted their manners, dressed like them, spoke with their accent and learnt their language and jokes. The grammar school boy who came up [to Oxford] to sit for scholarship exams with fountain pen clipped into his breast pocket, in school blazer... would change the way he dressed in order to conform. *If he learned, to adapt* no one cared what school he had gone to."[49] As seen here, it was a one-way street with the grammar-school student aping his "betters" in line with the English class system.

The mass of the English school-age population, each generation gets looked over and left out, even today, despite vigorous noises from the Establishment that it is not so. Unlike the rich and technologically advanced countries of the West, including the United States, Japan, and Germany, the world's economic Big Three Powers, England only allows less than 20 percent of its people to have a university education, as compared to 60 percent in the leading nations—the Big Three—with France, Canada, and Italy comparable or less, but above England, the most feudal of the seven nations mentioned. Many children drop out of school at age sixteen and do not ever receive any kind of technical training, as they do in Germany, in such fields as electricity, mechanics, plumbing, and carpentry.

In a report by Chris Woodhead, Chief Inspector of Schools, it was revealed that "white boys" from poor inner city schools are at the bottom of the educational pile, below girls and ethnic minorities.[50] Since England has a 90 to 95 percent white population and an 80 percent working-class population, this figure of poorly educated white boys has to be very large indeed. Meanwhile, the chief inspector of schools does not offer any reasons as to why this fail-

---

[49] Annan, pp. 11–12.
[50] "Under Pressure" by Linda Grant, *Guardian*, March 11, 1996, pp. 6–7.

ure exists among English white school boys. He fails to identify the class system, which reinforces a large underclass each generation, as a possible reason for this lack of educational attainment among many of England's young. With an Establishment, which has historically disdained business and engineering as unworthy professions for a Gentleman, the incentive among the indigenous population to be creative and enterprising in an economic structure comparatively static is minimal. New jobs and forms of employment, new possibilities for advancement in life are not a reality for the vast number of English people. The financial capital needed for expansion mostly lies within the Establishment, who historically invest it abroad for a greater return rather than at home.

The "outsiders' view," again, bears out the truth, now in the English educational ethic. "The real class division—I would even say class antagonism—in Britain today is between the public-school Oxbridge elite and everybody else on down… This Establishment… [is] instilled presumably at a young age at school, with a firm sense of their own moral and intellectual superiority. It is the Establishment [as few as six thousand people superimposed on 53 million people], or public school Oxbridge elite, which makes Britain seem so small and focused… They constantly air their ideas in books, newspaper columns, reviews and television chat shows."[51] Besides the foreign office, the home office, the treasury, the City of London, Oxford and Cambridge, the public schools, the military, and personal service to the Royal Family, other members of the elite go into the agencies of propaganda, the media, advertising, and the arts. They shape how the rest of the world sees England, including the Americans. At the top are the professional managers or "mandarins" who move with ease throughout English institutions, managing a ministry or an embassy abroad, a bank or an Oxford college, a television channel or a newspaper, even the Royal Opera at Covent Garden. All totalitarian societies in history, particularly in this century, have functioned similarly, but with not nearly the success or ease of the crafty English Establishment. Critchfield goes on to say, "A few gifted

---

[51] Critchfield, pp. 59–60.

non-Oxbridge people are let in from time to time. But participation is not generally widened. *To make itself more democratic would be to loosen the Oxbridge elite's grip on British society"* and therefore the Establishment's!

And what do individual Englishmen think who have been to the country's most prestigious public school? Some express serious reservations about them, while many are normally impressed with them, and themselves, as is the rest of the population, surprisingly. *Eton Voices*, published in the 1980s, tells this story. Anthony Blond, the publisher of educational books, when discussing his house at Eton, said, "The house was run on terror, run on fear, definitely. Everybody was constantly in fear, fear of failing, fear of being sent down, fear of being beaten, fear, fear, fear. That's why they are so rough."[52] Who is "so rough"? The men of the Establishment, of course, and cruel. Bullying always has been, and still is, an accepted part of English education, perhaps a character-toughening exercise. Andrew Callender said of his Eton experience, "At Oxford you are an Etonian. Socially, everyone knows you're an Etonian,"[53] which begs the question, "In England, which is more important vis-á-vis society and the Establishment—going to Oxford or going to Eton?" (Going to Eton, naturally!)

Mark Fiennes reflected on Eton thus, "The Eton education gives you that confidence because it gives you certainty." However, it is only certainty for the very few. He then said, "But I think the thing I dislike about Eton most of all ["Don't say it too loud or all those middle-class parents with high aspirations for their sons might hear you!"]…is that it symbolises, it epitomises, the English hierarchical system, and God how the English love hierarchy. *Although they say they don't,* although they may bitch and whinge behind the scenes [more English pantomime]…they love the forelock-touching and the kow-towing. You can see it in their adulation of royalty; because there is no God in England any more, royalty are the dynasty, they are the people that symbolise the system right the way down through

---

[52] Danzinger, D (ed) <u>Eton Voices,</u> London, 1988 (p 47)
[53] Ibid (p 65)

the Right Honourable this, and the Lady that and the Lord this."[54] Of course, has anything really changed in this social structure since early Anglo-Saxon times, and when did the English really, fervently believe in God, except prior to the Reformation and briefly in the seventeenth century, when the devout few finally emigrated to New England. What other country in the world uses as quasi-sacred texts *Debrett's Correct Form* and *Debrett's Peerage*, and actually takes them seriously, at least within the Establishment.

Finally, what happens when things go wrong in paradise, when the system backfires, or at least, sputters because some members betray it, such as the Oxford and Cambridge Communist spies of this century. James Lee-Milne in his autobiography *Another Self* disdained the conduct of some of his contemporaries who indulged in such unorthodox politics. He wrote, "For while I was at Oxford many undergraduates were fellow travellers. Others became party members... They came from comfortable middle-class backgrounds. They were the intellectual elite of the university in the early thirties... Their potential superiority made a defection from the long tradition of European civilisation all the more loathsome... Their fanaticism helped to contribute to the present-day falsification of political arguments, distortion of basic truths and a depreciation of civilised values."[55] Maybe so. Although the potential and practice of deceit and falsehood has been inherent in English institutions for centuries, it is only that most people have turned a blind eye to them or chosen to think the best of their country. What prompted the Oxford and Cambridge public school educated, middle-class intellectuals to betray their country and "its values"? Some say it was prompted by the emergence of America as the world's dominant power, a liberal, bourgeois middle-class democracy, "for the people, by the people and of the people," so contrary to the values of the English class system and England's small ruling elite. Russian Communism, in practice, after all, was more akin to the elitist ideals such as the English public-school boys knew and respected so dearly from their earliest

---

[54] Ibid (p 91)
[55] Lees-Milne, J <u>Another Self</u>, First published 1970, London 1984 (p 95–96)

indoctrination into them. While America preached personal freedom and liberty, England preached a creed closer to that of Czarist as well as Communist Russia. Perhaps the English Communist spies of the twentieth century were more loyal to the values of their own country than one cares to realize or admit.

CHAPTER VII

Ethics in the Workplace: Promises and Pleasures

The Protestant work ethic, identified by the English historian, R. H. Tawney and, earlier, by the German economist Max Weber in his essay "The Protestant Ethic and the Spirit of Capitalism" gave rise to an academic discussion in the West, still not resolved as to the influence of Protestantism on capitalism and the subsequent industrial revolution in England in the late eighteenth century. Tawney acknowledged his debt to Weber's essay in pointing out the relationship between religion and social theory.[56] He believed, however, that Weber oversimplified "the capitalist spirit" and "Protestant ethics," and their close relationship, by saying they "were a good deal more complex than Weber seems to imply."[57] Here, the English historian blows his horn regarding the earlier historical discoveries of the German economist. But Tawney went on to say, "What is true and valuable in his essay is his insistence that the commercial classes in seventeenth century England were the standard bearers of a particular conception of social expediency, which was markedly different from that of the more conservative elements in society—the peasants, the craftsmen and many landed gentry—and that that conception found

---

[56] Tawney, R. H., *Religion and the Rise of Capitalism*, New York, 1926, p. 261.
[57] Ibid., p. 262.

expression in religion, in politics and...in social and economic conduct and policy."[58] Initially, then England led the Western world in the ways of capitalism, with individuals and groups of Englishmen, investing large sums of money in various explorations abroad while tapping the natural resources of these new found lands, accruing great profits for the original investors back home through the intricacies of commerce. Such money amassed in the early Protestant centuries in England was available for investing in machinery when the industrial revolution dawned in England, fueled by the discovery of coal and expedited by the invention of the railways. A new, although, very small middle class sprang up in England during these years of economic change. By Victorian times, these new rich industrialists were on the verge of reshaping English life and values, spurred on by the Protestant work ethic.

The Old Establishment sensed what was about to take place and recoiled in horror. They ingeniously began recruiting the sons of the industrial middle class by allowing them entrance to the public schools, where they were indoctrinated against the crass commercialism and philistine ways of their nouveau rich families. Held up to these middle-class sons instead were the aristocratic ideals, embodied in the English Gentleman. To work with one's hands, whether manually or managerially in a factory, would never do for a Gentleman. "The children of businessmen were admitted to full membership in the upper class, at the price of discarding the distinctive, production-oriented culture shaped during [the past century, 1750–1850]." These children forsook the industrial town for the country estate. "The adoption of a culture of enjoyment by the new landowners... meant the dissipation of a set of values that had projected their fathers as a class to the economic heights, and the nation to world predominance." This new ideal for the new landowners, the Gentleman, was "the older aristocratic ideal purged of its grosser elements by the nineteenth century religious revival. Indeed, Bertrand Russell— himself a hereditary peer—was to suggest that 'the concept of the Gentleman was invented by the aristocracy to keep the middle classes

---

[58] Ibid., pp. 262–263.

in order.'"[59] Thus, the triumph of the English middle class, which seemed inevitable in the 1830s and 1840s, came to a crashing halt, eventually dragging down the economic progress of the English people, whose country by 1870 was already being surpassed by Germany and the United States.

As Max Weber pointed out in his essay on the Protestant work ethic, the only real resilience in the English economic system, going back a few centuries, were the small commercial classes, who were finally kept in check by 1850 by the rest of society pulling together against them, led by the gentry and aristocracy, *and supported in this conservative reactionary movement by the working classes.* This historic alliance between the rich and the working poor in England conspired against progress in all areas of English life, including the work place. Joined together with them were the intellectual classes. The noted Victorian authors, including Anthony Trollope, John Ruskin, the later Charles Dickens, and Matthew Arnold, whose father Thomas Arnold gave a great boost to the public school ethos, including the concept of the Christian Gentleman, decried the corrupting influence of commercialism upon "an older quasi-feudal society." "Even John Stuart Mill, the foremost 'philosophic radical' at mid-century, felt the qualms of a Gentleman...in the face of the material preoccupations of early Victorian England."[60] Thomas Carlyle, a one-time friend of Mills, declared that the business of life is not business, and that the *work ethic* was not the core of morality.[61] The working classes continued to hold on to a vision of "Merrie England," perhaps prompted by such middle-class, nineteenth-century socialists as William Morris, Edward Carpenter, and Robert Blatchford, who denounced industrialism and commercialism in favor of a pastoral life, such as they imagined to have existed in England centuries earlier, with images of the happy and contented peasant.[62]

---

[59] Wiener, M. J., *English Culture and the Decline of the Industrial Spirit, 1850–1980*, Cambridge University Press, 1981, p. 13.

[60] Wiener, p. 32.

[61] Ibid., p. 32.

[62] Ibid., p. 119.

The American historian Martin Wiener's conclusions about English culture and decline are mostly dismissed by the Establishment today as nonsense and a bad dream. He may have come too close to the truth, which makes the ruling class uneasy and fearful of losing their control on society and power. Noel Annan suggested that Our Age was made very uneasy by Wiener's indictment of the English class system as responsible for England's economic decline up to the present day. Together with Correlli Barnett, whom Annan called "the Jeremiah of his generation," the Establishment merely sputters and puffs when confronted with their arguments regarding England's decline. Like so many creatures of the English Establishment, Noel Annan effectively lists all the criticisms levelled against Our Age, but he never seriously refutes them or comes up with an alternative as to what really went wrong. To do so, he would betray his class, which he is loath to do. But not to do so, he betrays England and the English people who ought to know the truth. Rather, Annan and his group would rather attack the critics personally as being unworthy of the gentlemanly ideal, saying of Barnett and by association Wiener, that they "were willing to throw into the trash can humanism, liberalism and parliamentarism as luxuries that [England] could no longer afford if she was to become efficient."[63] As a typical Establishment argument, he does not explain what he means by these "-isms" and fully expects his readers to shrink back in horror at the thought of losing them. That something more human and all embracing, such as personal freedom and liberty, are still missing in English life he does not say.

Martin Wiener came to his own conclusion about England's industrial and economic decline, regardless of any offence it might cause to the English Establishment. He wrote, "The social and intellectual revolution implicit in industrialism was muted, perhaps even aborted. Instead a compromise was effected...a synthesis of old and new. This containment of the cultural revolution of industrialism lies at the heart of both the achievements and the failures of modem British history... In particular, the later nineteenth century

---

[63] Annan, p. 454.

saw the consolidation of a national élite:… It administered the most extensive empire in human history with reasonable effectiveness and humanity, and it maintained a remarkable degree of political and social stability at home… It also presided over the steady erosion of the nation's economic position in the world."[64]

Correlli Barnett, an Englishman, does not always take such a charitable view of his own country's achievements in terms of Empire and social stability at home. He particularly attacks the myth of the English war effort from 1939 to 1945, so popularized as a most wonderful time for English people coming together by such people as Elizabeth, the Queen Mother. His first book *The Audit of War* published in 1986 showed a picture of maximum dependency on American industry because English industry was plagued by wildcat strikes and managed by the other worldly members of the upper class, whose true ambition was not to make profits but to have enough time and money to live the lives of English Gentlemen. In his most recent book, Barnett said England squandered valuable Marshall Aid money from the United States, following the conclusion of the Second World War by trying to "play the squire" on the world stage, deluding itself and, hopefully, the rest of the world that it was one of the Big Three Powers, together with the United States and the former Soviet Union. While receiving more Marshall Aid than any other European nation, the English Establishment used it to prop up the pound sterling, to hold on to the Empire, together with English military and naval power, and to establish the welfare state to appease and once again check the working classes. He wrote, "In the 1960s and 1970s British folk-wisdom cherished (perhaps still cherishes) a comfortable explanation for Britain's relative economic decline since the Second World War… West Germany, the story goes, had all her industries and transport systems bombed flat during the war, and then, thanks to Marshall Aid was able completely to rebuild them with the most up-to-date equipment. Meanwhile, poor old Britain had to struggle on with worn-out and obsolete kit. This favourite British 'wooden leg' excuse [among many others] is pure myth."

---

[64] Wiener, pp. 157–158.

In fact, Barnett pointed out the German industrial capacity in 1948 stood at 90 percent of 1936. Next to Germany's $1.7-billion aid, Britain received $2.7 billion. The Labour government, upon the advice of its economists, chose not to make the re-equipping of England as an industrial society the priority use of the Marshall Aid. "Instead, the government saw Marshall Aid (like the American loan of 1945 [$3.5 billion at 2 percent per annum until 1951]) primarily as a wad of greenbacks stuffed by kindly Uncle Sam into the breeches pocket of a nearly bankrupt John Bull who, though diligently seeking future solvency, nevertheless still wished in the meantime to go on playing the squire, beneficent to his *family* and the *poor*, and grand among the neighbours."[65]

Correlli Barnett's other major criticism of the English Establishment's handling of the immediate post-war economy is the reluctance to improve practices and procedures, let alone equipment in the manufacturing and business sectors. So imbued with its sense as the center of the universe, presided over by Gentlemen, where "England is time," a dual policy of "make-do and mend" in manufacturing and "take it or leave it" in business only helped to push England over the edge into serious economic difficulties. Already, it has been seen that the Marshall Aid money, which Germany and France used to rebuild and update their industrial plants, was squandered by the English government on loftier concerns. Now any money for such purposes had to be raised solely from the English business community itself. This economic post-war tack depended mostly on English business being willing to be competitive in the world markets, particularly in the United States, the sole victor of the war that just ended. The gentlemen of English business instead turned their noses at such a notion of producing goods in England that would be competitive in American markets, even though such goods appealing to American tastes probably would fill the coffers of English industry. Meanwhile traditional English customers complained now of the lofty, inefficient treatment they received from English manufacturers. "'The policy of 'take it or leave it' is quite outplayed in

---

[65] Barnett, C., *The Lost Victory*, London, 1995, p. 365.

the Swiss market, where the client insists on service and delivery to specification... Failure to keep promised delivery dates, non-observance of Swiss buying seasons, unforeseen additional charges, abnormal packing expenses, delays in replying to enquiries...and apparent disinterestedness in the little market, have turned away many a good post-war client who now looks elsewhere for his needs.'"[66] The sheer arrogance of English business in manufacturing goods according to its own sense of excellence, and "expecting the customer to gratefully buy it" can only be the product of a society so used to telling an underclass what to do that when confronted with the real world of democratic peoples, the English are at a loss. More comfortable are they in dealing within the Commonwealth, or in countries that have a lower standard of living than their own. Anyone who does business in England, even today, knows that most of these same criticisms can be made. Barnett concluded, "Surely it was beyond the wit of men, certainly Birmingham or Manchester men, to abandon the British version as quickly as practicable in favour of making American types, which in any case would have very likely gone down better with European customers like the Swiss as well."[67]

Nick Leeson, the disgraced Barings Bank "rogue trader" knows all too well, better than the Establishment bosses for whom he once worked, that money makes the world go round, generated by hard work and the willing adaptability of the work force, together with the business leaders for whom they work. He expressed amazement in a recent autobiographical account of his part in the collapse of London's oldest merchant bank, when the chairman of Barings, Peter Baring, discussed so casually in 1993 with Brian Quinn, the director of the Bank of England in charge of all banking supervision, the ease of making money in the securities business. Thinking that all was well in Singapore under Nick Leeson's management of the Barings Bank operation in SIMEX, not knowing about his employee's 88888 account, hiding enormous losses out of sight from the internal auditors eyes, he "laconically commented: 'the recovery in profitability

---

[66] Ibid., p. 381.
[67] Ibid., p. 383.

has been amazing following the re-organisation, leaving Barings to conclude that it was not *actually terribly difficult* to make money in the securities business.'"[68]

Leeson, coming from a working-class family in Watford, by his own admission, combined both "a swat and a lad." He expressed disdain for his upper-class masters in the banking world and understandably has difficulty, matching the right intonation of Peter Barings' words "'not actually terribly difficult.'" Such are the apparent subtleties and cruel after effects of the English class system upon many such people in England. Leeson went on to say, "They should have known better. Certainly Peter Baring should have known better. Making money is never easy—his ancestors who built the bank and took risks and went out to visit canals and railways, would never have said that making money was 'not actually terribly difficult'. Nobody in the real world thinks that making money is not actually terribly difficult."[69] Is the English Establishment in the real world of which Peter Baring was once a member in good standing, and probably still is? It seems unlikely that any group that still thinks in terms of a ruling-class ethic, and is so reluctant to surrender this pretense—and all the trappings it provides for the individuals within its cozy core, even at the expense of their nation's economic decline—is surely not in the real world of any age, let alone the world of today. The particular culture Nick Leeson grew up in is more real, with its ethic of work and survival in a class-ridden society. He wrote, "My father knows that you have to work hard and that you get paid £20 a square yard for plastering and that you've got to keep the customers happy to get referred on. The laundry on the corner, the boy who delivers newspapers, the lawyer working above the estate agency just on the wrong end of the high street—they all know that making money is never easy."[70]

In England, unfortunately, the people who count, who have the most to say, who run the show, have little concern for making

---

[68] Leeson, N., with Edward Whitley, *Rogue Trader*, London, 1996, p. 72.
[69] Ibid., p. 73.
[70] Ibid., p. 23.

money and know little therefore that hard work is required to do so. That effortless ease of the English Gentleman, so cherished as an ideal by the Establishment, has a corrupting influence on all aspects of economic life in England, particularly on those individuals who accept and aspire to this ideal. Their number is legion, whether they are working class, middle class, or unemployed. Instead, the English work for the enjoyment of their pleasures, as Nick Leeson gave his reader a glimpse of such pursuits in his story about Barings. How unlike they are from the Germans and the Americans, the two people the English Establishment despise the most, who work to create something new, who work to advance themselves economically and technologically, and therefore, advance their nations. In contrast, how precious are the gentlemen's clubs to the English, the formal dinners and dances, the exclusiveness of Glyndebourne (an annual summer Festival Opera in East Sussex), the games like polo that only gentlemen can afford to play and appreciate.

When Barings Bank collapsed in February 1995, the Establishment rallied round its members, fearing that a blow to one venerable institution might expose the rest of them to national censor and, worst still, loss of power. Leeson noted that "life as a banker in the rarefied circles of the Bank of England was so different from my life in Singapore. In their high vaulted offices along Cheapside, Peter Baring could talk of it being 'not actually terribly difficult to make money in securities', or Christopher Thompson [the senior manager of the Bank of England in charge of supervising merchant banks such as Barings] could apologise that something was 'buried reasonably deep in his in-tray' [regarding Barings exceeding the 25 percent limit in Far East markets thereby exposing its capital] as if this was perfectly acceptable. The Bank of England gave tacit approval for Barings to transfer more than 25% of its share capital with little more than a nod and a wink."[71] For all these reasons of wanting to protect its own, Nick Leeson believes that the serious fraud office chose not to have him tried in England, preferring the distance a Singapore trial would provide for the interests of the Establishment.

---

[71] Ibid., p. 97.

Meanwhile, the conservative leaning newspaper, the *Daily Telegraph*, seemed to get as good a grip on what happened between Nick Leeson and the Establishment as any commentary on this shocking financial episode—a modem English class drama. On July 18, the Bank of England issued its final report on the collapse of Barings Bank. The *Telegraph*'s editorial read, "'The report reflects badly on the Bank of England, badly on Mr Leeson, but worst of all on the senior management of Barings. It defies comprehension... that a single individual could have wreaked havoc for almost 3 years without detection. Mr Leeson is neither a victim nor a hero, merely the latest in a long history of young men entrusted with responsibility for which they proved unfit. But it is those who sat on the board of Barings who emerge from this story as almost sublime incompetents, blithely counting their own booty on the promenade deck, oblivious to the torrent cascading into their ship below the waterline... If Mr Leeson goes to prison while the former board of Barings continues to go to Glyndebourne, this sorry saga will leave the bitterest of tastes.'"[72]

The words of this editorial from the *Daily Telegraph* have been fulfilled and probably still go unheeded by the powers that be. Meanwhile at home, in August 1996, a government report showed that 7.6 percent of the workforce was unemployed with 2.1 million people claiming unemployment insurance. Also, 228,000 workdays were lost in June due to strikes and illnesses. And in comparison with economies abroad, the United States was leading the world in terms of new job creation with unemployment at 5.2 percent.[73] The gap between the rich and the poor is four times, or more, higher than the average income of the poor in Brazil, Britain, and Guatemala, according to the Human Development Report 1996, compiled by the UN Development Program.[74] Finally, a report published by the Government's statistical service recently showed that "most of the

---

[72] Ibid., p. 252.

[73] "When it Comes to Job Creation America Wins Hands Down," *Times*, October 15, 1996, p. 31.

[74] "UN Finds Worlds of Rich and Poor Widening," *International Herald Tribune*, July 16, 1996, p. 6.

United Kingdom is poorer than the rest of the European Union, and only the South East and East Anglia are wealthier than the continental average... The UK has the ninth highest gross income per head in the [fifteen-member] Union... Only Sweden, Finland, Ireland, Spain, Portugal and Greece are poorer."[75] The richest area in the EU is Hamburg in Germany!

The conclusions from all these statistics and surveys seems obvious. Past experience reveals that the Establishment, and all who support it, believe only what they want to believe. They seem to be quite content to go: "Row, row, row your boat gently down the stream. Merrily, merrily, merrily, merrily, life is but a dream." The real world of economic reality is not for the English Gentleman. He remains the creature of a static worldview in which his country is believed to be in full control, so that everything can be paced according to *the English way of life*—that is, the life of England's elite. This view of England in the world continues to be yet one more "dream" translated as lie, which the Establishment refuses to surrender despite facts to the contrary.

---

[75] "Poor Man of Europe Lags Behind Continent," *Times*, June 26, 1996, p. 7.

CHAPTER VIII

Ethics in Sports: Jolly Good Fun

The Conservative English politician, Enoch Powell, is quoted as saying in 1976, "The life of a nation no less than that of men is lived largely in the imagination."[76] Surely, no nation in the Western world fulfils this description of its life than England, where the most important thing is in the doing of something, in the form, while content and results take a back seat. Not least, is this priority to good form found in English sports, at least, traditionally those played by Gentlemen. Like everything else in English life, class is the final arbiter in deciding who plays what, where, and when. The 10 percent of students who attend private, fee-paying schools in England usually play competitively three games, depending on the season of the year, rugby or rugger football, rowing, and cricket. While other games may be played informally among the boys, such as the Eton Wall Game or soccer, Gentlemen participate in only the big three. The game of soccer, England's national sport, is played by mostly working-class boys, who one day, may become players on one of the big national teams, or even on England's team. Less rarely, there are crowd disturbances at rugby games, rowing tournaments, and cricket matches, while the phenomenon of "football hooliganism" has arisen in the past half century, particularly in the outdated soccer stadiums throughout the land supported primarily by working-class fans watching work-

---

[76] Wiener, frontispiece.

ing-class players. Surely, it is quite a different experience from a day watching cricket at Lord's.

Since England is best, the English like to think their country should win over all others when competing on the international athletic stage. When England loses, the winners are usually blamed. What seems so lacking in English sport, whether it is played between schools, national, or international teams, is the absence of the American sporting ethic—may the best man win. As a predominantly middle-class country with first-class stadiums, sport is a family outing in the United States, complete with marching bands, as well as half-time shows for football games and the seventh inning stretch for baseball games. While riots can and do occur after England's soccer matches, with its nearly 100 percent working-class male fans fighting among themselves or causing public damage, American families leave their sports stadiums happily after games, having had a nice day out, and maybe, even their favorite team winning.

Perhaps just to see what might happen in England if football, American style, was played in English soccer stadiums before English fans, complete with cheerleaders and half-time shows, English observers are amazed that the fans behave more like polite bourgeois Americans instead of rowdy lower-class Englishmen. The setting for one particular American football game was held in London at Stamford Bridge. Described as "a bleak, warlike place: part stadium, part fortress," it sounds well-suited as a complement to the historic martial spirit of the English. One sports writer said, "It often rains here, but it doesn't only rain; visiting fans have known it to rain darts and razor-like sharpened coins. During the soccer season, the Chelsea head-hunters, one of the capital's most feared hooligan 'firms', are known to frequent Stamford Bridge."[77] But seated there, to the writer's amazement, were his "Americanised compatriots," drinking cans of beer with no apparent inclination to throw them as missiles as would inevitably happen during an English soccer game; hence, alcohol is never allowed on the premises for such events.

---

[77] "A Bloody Good Game" by Sam Willetts, *American Way* (American Airlines flight magazine), October 15, 1996, p. 51.

While there is now a world football league, the WLAF (World League of American Football) with six teams from London, Scotland, Reims, Frankfurt, Amsterdam, and Barcelona, the London Monarchs are mostly unknown to the English public and treated with indifference by the English media. About 11,000 fans come out to the stadiums to watch them play, such as at Stamford Bridge. "Anti-football types in the United Kingdom dislike what they see as an attempted cultural invasion. In London many fans want to be American for an afternoon, to escape from English glumness and inhibition... The fact is—and this says a lot about football's appeal over here—everybody seemed happy."[78]

In contrast to these American niceties in the world of sport, English fans and the English press behaved with particular vengeance and cruelty during the June 1996 World Soccer Championship Finals between Germany and England. Some people commented that the atmosphere in the country suggested that World War II was about to be fought all over again. Before the Euro '96 Games even began, with sixteen national teams participating, an American sports writer wrote of it as follows: "Einstein's theory that nationalism is an infantile disease 'the measles of mankind' might explain why the world is so open to the spread of soccer."[79] That country in the West, which can be most infantile when it comes to national pride was evident during those games. Despite voices of protest from the German press regarding the bellicose stance the English press had affected toward the World soccer finals, the English were typically unrepentant as a superior people who could never be wrong, or at least, found out to be wrong.

The conservative MP, John Redwood, a onetime challenger for the premiership of John Major, recalled all the past English prejudices and hatreds toward the efficient and prosperous German nation in a newspaper article coinciding with the Euro '96 finals. He wrote, "England's football fixture against Germany has raised more than

---

[78] Ibid., p. 127.
[79] "The World Will Focus on this Ball" by Rob Hughes, *International Herald Tribune*, June 8–9, 1996, p. 1.

the usual hyperbole, lurid headlines and hot air. There is something special about the contest. It has stirred deep feelings. It invites us to think again about the *problem of Germany*. The German question has bedevilled Europe in the twentieth century."[80] How a game of soccer between two national teams can be whipped into a political problem concerning the stronger soccer team, only the English are capable of doing without blushing or feeling in the least bit hypocritical. Only by reading the last paragraph will the reader learn that John Redwood was "only joking" about what he had just said about "the German problem." Or was he just playing the game of English ethics? "Football is a good way of letting off steam. We should remember it is only a game. It is good *sometimes* to ask basic questions about Britain's relationship with Germany."[81]

When England was inevitably defeated by Germany in the soccer finals, even the neighboring Scots were reported as cheering in their pubs north of the border as another blow to English pride in the world was dealt to them. Critics from the American press declared it was time for England to grow up and stop its tantrums. Headlines in the English press such as "Let's Blitz Fritz" and proclamations of a "football war" on Germany was seen as "a far cry from a country that was once proud of the gentlemanly maxim: 'It's not winning but how you play the game that counts.'"[82]

Meanwhile, England in defeat, merely turned all the proper criticism against its team upside down. They had seemingly lost a holy war to the detriment of the world's freedom. One newspaper reported on its front page, "*The hopes and prayers of a nation* were shattered last night when England was beaten by Germany in a thrilling semi-final of Euro '96 at Wembley."[83] The article continued in typical melodramatic style, "The result came as a horrible anti-cli-

[80] "Stand up to Germany, on and off the field" by John Redwood, *Times*, June 26, 1996, p. 20.

[81] Ibid., p. 20.

[82] "Britain Must Grow Up and Stop the Tantrums" by Flora Lewis, *International Herald Tribune*, June 27, 1996, p. 1.

[83] "It's All Over for England" by Ben Fenton and Robert Hardman, *Daily Telegraph*, June 27, 1996, p. 1.

max to the hordes of fans at Wembley and *to the nation as a whole.* [England's finest hour seemed about to be re-enacted all over again!] Days of burgeoning hope were cast into darkest night at the end of a game of incredible excitement and then almost unbearable tension."

Unlike the calm and happy fans of a defeated team at America's annual Super Bowl, the defeated English fans "went on a rampage of Trafalgar Square. Youths hurled hundreds of bottles during confrontations with riot police, who mounted two baton charges. Several people were treated for cuts. Late last night 500 strong group of youths broke away from the Square and set fire to a sports car and overturned a third. A police car was also damaged and other cars had their windscreens broken. Bedfordshire and Thames Valley police also reported vandalism and violence by drunken youths."[84] For the English fans, of course, it was all in a typical night's fun—almost "jolly good fun," except the fans' accents were not quite right.

The *Times* newspaper tried to be less subjective than its sister paper the *Daily Telegraph* in its "final analysis" of Euro '96, typed out in very fine print! It said of Germany that they did everything right off the field and, on the field "were always trying to go for victory," as if the other fifteen participating teams, including England, did not want to win, just "play the game." Finally, the analysis said, "Their athleticism and organisation took them through—*a role model for England to copy.* German teams in the past have demanded respect; this team deserves to be remembered with affection, too."[85] Buried away in the sports section of the newspaper, it is doubtful that many people in England read those words. The last thing the English would want to do, based upon their past utterances and behavior, would be to take any people as a role model, except dead people like the Romans, but most surely not the Germans.

The next day, the *Daily Telegraph* bounced back and saved the day for English pride once again. By not showing boring "professionalism" like other teams, with "its dark and devious face" the defeated English soccer team heralded a new day for sport, where the fans at

---

[84] Fenton and Hardman, *Daily Telegraph*, p. 1.
[85] "Euro 96 The Final Analysis," *Times*, July 1, 1996, p. 31.

Wembley saw "the rebirth of the heroic spirit of daring" with its "disdain of caution."[86] And yet the English have always styled themselves before the world, especially before the more "impetuous" Americans, as a cautious people. Indeed, the English like to turn the world upside down *if it suits them.*

More bad news for England's athletes was to come almost a month later from the Summer Olympic Games in Atlanta, Georgia. Here, they were not even accorded the honor of gaining entrance to any semi-finals, except for the rare individual effort, when a piece of gold and silver came their way. At the end of these games, Great Britain brought home fifteen medals—one gold, eight silver, six bronze. It ranked seventeenth out of seventy-eight nations which won any medals at the Games, while countries like Ethiopia, Algeria, Norway, and Sweden won twice as much gold as did the United Kingdom (English, Scottish, Welsh, and Northern Irish athletes combined). The English turned out to be bad or sore losers, as they did off the record and the field following their Euro '96 defeat. Good sportsmanship, at the least, has always demanded that the athlete be a good loser, especially at the world's premier athletic contest. Being a crafty people, the English Establishment turned their defeat and another country's victory upside down, on its head, mirroring their unsportsmanlike performance following the June 1996 soccer finals.

No nation in the history of the Olympic Games since their modern beginning in Athens in 1896 has achieved more success than the United States of America. Half the Olympic gold medals have gone to the Americans over the years. No nation comes close to this achievement. With the collapse of the Soviet Union, various countries like the Ukraine and Belorussia, nine in all, entered the Olympic Games for the first time in Atlanta as separate nations, each with its own team. The English press chose to stomp on the American victory with a similar vitriolic spirit as they attacked Germany during the Euro '96 Games. According to their tabulations, adding Russia and its nine former dependencies' medal count together, a grand total of

---

[86] "Three Cheers for Our Jolly Good Sports" by Harry Eyres, *Daily Telegraph*, July 2, 1996, p. 15.

114 medals were won by the former Soviet Communists. This calculation would push the United States into second place with only 101
medals. Despite this devious English move, the United States still led
in the number of gold medals—43 to 38.

If that was not enough to deflate the American victory, as if the
United States had won for the first time, the English "turning the
tables" trick can be used. When dividing a country's population by
the number of medals it won, the United States came out in thirtieth
place, behind the British Commonwealth countries of New Zealand,
Australia, and Canada, with New Zealand the "new winner" of the
Atlanta Games. Sadly for England, it came out even lower following
this population calculation than on the medal count tally per nation,
ranking in thirty-eighth, rather than seventeenth place.[87]

Why do the English bother with such petty nonsense? Why are
they so envious of America's first place in the world of nations? Why
do they snuggle so close to the former totalitarian Soviet State, as if
hoping, somehow, it was still a superpower pitted against the United
States? The answer to these questions are obvious in coming to a better understanding of English ethics herein being exposed.

Another predictable English way of attacking an adversary, in
the case of the United States and its Olympic team, is to go for a
kind of character assassination. This method effectively removes
criticism from the English and their Olympic team by brutally
and persistently criticizing the host nation, which happens to be
England's oldest adversary, dating back to 1776, long before the
"German threat" loomed large in the mid-nineteenth century. The
initial object of England's Olympic attack this particular year was
the fledgling city of Atlanta, for the first time an Olympic city, having beaten out England's own Manchester in the selection process.
It was first, and always, the heat of Atlanta the English media kept
reminding its audiences each day during the Olympic Games that
was so unconducive to the performance of English athletes, not, of
course, taking into account that many of the nations participating

---

[87] "Soviet Echo as Successor States Rule Awards Table" by Richard Beeston in
Moscow, *Times*, August 5, 1996, p. 7.

have climates much hotter and more humid than Atlanta's summertime. The suggestion was made that the promoters of the Atlanta Games had lied about their summer temperatures to the Olympic Committee, which selected the site for the Games. This ruse used to berate Atlanta ignores the infamous English summers, which can be mostly rain, not exactly ideal for track and field events, as well as many others played mostly outside. Besides, has not the world come to believe that the English can endure any climate's conditions and "take no notice of it" for "only mad dogs and Englishmen go out in the midday sun!"

Next, to Atlanta's discredit, was the poor organization of transportation for the athletes from the Olympic village to the various sporting facilities and events. Loudest among all these critics amongst the world's athletes was England's sole gold medal winner, Steven Redgrave, who was described by his fellow oarsman, Matthew Pinsent, as being generally "bloody-minded." He bore Great Britain's flag in the Olympic Parade at the opening ceremonies, when the British team chose to be different from the rest, especially from the Americans who were made to "look like a mass audition for the Boy Friend"; instead, the British team "eschew[ed] the traditional blazer-and-tie routine." No other European country chose to be so bold. Instead, the British team, probably as a last-minute decision in Atlanta's heat, wore mostly shorts and open shirts, with wide brim hats, all designed by the Japanese-owned Aquascutum in London. "On Redgrave came, the grip not shifting. Others tried to carry the flag single-handed but were changing over long before the end… When Redgrave finally placed the flag all the officials shook his hand."[88] English superiority, however, did not bear out in the rest of the Games. English petulance and poor sportsmanlike attitudes surfaced with each passing day in Atlanta, signaling a proud nation's "Olympic shame," the worst performance by a British team since 1952, when it was blamed on Britain's recovery from the Second World War.

---

[88] "Opening Gambit Strikes Gold in Memorable Style" by Brough Scott in Atlanta, *Sunday Telegraph*, July 21, 1996, p. 53.

Despite his sour public persona and his unsportsmanlike attitudes toward his Olympic accomplishments, vowing in a television interview after his recent victory never to get into a boat again or else be shot, Steven Redgrave had to carry the sporting pride of his nation throughout the Games, beyond the opening ceremony, while ducking out of the closing ceremony. A sports writer for the *Times* hailed Redgrave, and therefore, the Englishman, as the Greatest Olympic athlete of all times. For him to win four gold medals in four consecutive Games, 1984–1996, "Redgrave thus joins three men with the same honour: [a Hungarian for fencing, a Dane for yachting, and an American for discus]." The American, Al Oerter, met Redgrave "to add his congratulations to the others *pouring in from around the world*. With no disrespect to the other three monumental achievers, *Redgrave's is perhaps supreme*. The disciplines of [the other three men] are primarily technical. So it is in rowing, yet under the added stresses of physical extremes that send the heartbeat racing towards 200 per minute. Here is one of the most violent of muscular sports…"[89]

When an English athlete did fall short of winning a gold medal, as they all did but one, and secured a silver one instead, as did Roger Black in the four hundred-meter race behind Michael Johnson of the United States, the silver came to be translated by the English press as "just as good as gold." After all, if glory went to Johnson, who predictably won again the Olympic track race, then *honor* went to Black, winning his first Olympic medal ever after a long succession of injuries beginning in 1987. "If one wished to tell one's grandchild a morality tale, it would be of Black's silver medal."[90] Apparently this sports writer believes that for the Englishman honor is a higher achievement than glory—and all this piousness coming from the "Land of Hope and Glory"!

A final English response to defeat came when one of England's track star gold medal hopefuls, Linford Christie, was disqualified from the one hundred-meter race after two false starts. Christie

---

[89] "Redgrave Stands Supreme Among the Olympian Elite" by David Miller, *Times*, July 29, 1996, p. 26.

[90] "When Silver is as Good as Gold" by David Miller, *Times*, July 31, 1996, p. 42.

refused to accept the decision of the Olympic officials and kept the other seven finalists waiting "while consumed by his own self-importance. Even Mike Marsh, from the United States, normally the most placid and *honourable* of sprinters said: 'I very rarely think or say that somebody has acted immaturely, but Linford did. He demanded to come back into the race. That defied logic. This is the Olympics.'"[91]

Christie later commented that in England, he could have persuaded the judge to believe him and allow him to re-enter the race. But this time, he was in America, where the rules could not be bent. "'If it was anywhere else other than the USA, I am sure I would have been in', he said."[92] A few days later. in a postmortem on the British effort in Atlanta, all was forgiven by Simon Barnes, writing in the *Times*. Sport is really for pleasure. Only in totalitarian societies and places like [ugh!] the United States with its "college system" that "is open to abuses and corruption [whatever he means by all that!] is sport a serious matter." But not in good, olde England, where all those plucky Englishmen play the game for the pleasure of it. As for Linford Christie's disqualification [not to mention his initial defiance in refusing to accept the officials' decision in Atlanta], it was due to an "infinitesimal error—*an error of boldness.*" Therefore, there is no need for the English nation to fret and feel depressed about its poor showing. The higher ideals—English ideals—of sport are the most important—anti-professionalism; a heroic spirit of daring; honor, not glory; boldness; and pleasure.

Two days later, the *Times* editorial read, "Fool's Gold: Games are for players, not politicians and sportocrats." So what if Britain's medal score was a quarter of Germany's, a third of France's, half of Italy's?[93]

After all, America bashing (and German bashing) is more fun, "jolly good fun," rather like throwing bread rolls at an upper-class sports dinner or general public get-together, called fondly by the Establishment "a bun fight." The English press tells us that Atlanta's

---

[91] "Christie Mystery Comes to False End" by David Powell, *Times*, July 29, 1996, p. 23.

[92] Ibid., p. 23.

[93] "Fool's Gold" (editorial), *Times*, August 5, 1996, p. 17.

commercialism and greed tarnished the Olympic ideal.[94] The one-sided Olympic coverage in America by NBC was noted as "grotesquely distorted" in favor of the American teams and point of view. However, anyone watching the Olympic Games in England or Japan daily throughout the event easily noted that both nations' teams and points of view were presented mostly and, in England's case, sanctimoniously. "U! S! A! U! S! A!'. It is an anthem of superiority so baby-like, so irresistible and intimidating…that it reduces celebration to an unseemly metaphor for domination and chauvinism, and brings into question again the viability of the Olympics as a *healing force*… Linford Christie *was moved* to comment…that it seemed the Olympics didn't even exist for NBC if there was no American competing."[95] The English are adept at identifying their own shortcomings in other people's nations, while turning a blind eye to their own sins. Their coverage of the Atlanta Olympics was yet another case in point. From the looks on the faces of most English athletes during the Olympics, they appeared to be so happy to be participants in the world's greatest sporting competition that, like Atlanta, "they were too busy to hate." Their conduct should be a lesson to their countrymen that the freedom to be yourself—in America—surpasses the selfish pride and ethics of the English ruling class, more keen on national domination and glory than individual self-expression and liberty.

---

[94] "Greed Eclipses Olympic Creed at Atlanta 'Flea Market'" by Quentin Letts, *Times*, August 3, 1996, p. 13.

[95] "Raw Triumphalism and Now Pure Horror" by Kevin Mitchell, *Observer*, July 28, 1996, Sport p. 2.

CHAPTER IX

Ethics in Foreign Relations: This Seat of Mars

England's greatest PR man of all time is William Shakespeare. He is the only one the nation consistently points to as evidence that the English are a creative, literate, and civilized people. Yet this Bard from the Celtic regions and culture of England's island kingdom was able to point his finger at the most salient qualities of the native population. His many plays, comedies at first, and then with age and maturity, tragedies in great force, had very much to do with kings and queens, and all the capers they have always succeeded in getting up to, combining both humanity and power in these selected individuals. As Shakespeare indicates indirectly through his plays, and as any historian knows, so much of English history is about acts of cruelty and oppression, both at home and abroad over benighted peoples, performed by, or on behalf of, England's Monarchs. With irony, the playwright shines a light on England's contradictions in his play *Richard II*. The young king is portrayed as "a headstrong, passionate youth absorbed in degenerate expedients to get money for riot and finery," some would argue unhistorically so.[96] Nevertheless, the king's uncle, John of Gaunt, both extols England's attributes, as he understands them, and rails against foreign influences, indirectly attacking the strong French influence in his nephew's court. Such

---

[96] Shakespeare, W. (ed. Peter Ure), *King Richard II*, Arden Edition, London, 1956, p. 36.

foreign influences are corrupting the very Englishness of England. Gaunt declares these now famous words,

> This royal throne of kings, this scepter'd isle,
> This earth of majesty, this seat of Mars
> This other Eden, this demi-paradise,
> This fortress built by Nature for herself
> Against infection and the hand of war,
> This happy breed of men, this little world,
> This precious stone set in the silver sea,
> Which serves it in the office of a wall,
> Or as a moat defensive to a house,
> Against the envy of less happier lands,
> This blessed plot, this earth, this realm
> This England...[97]

A reading of these lines from William Shakespeare shows that nothing really has changed in English attitudes from then until today. The defining geographical characteristics in the English outlook is the island of Britain. It often prevents the English people from being more conversant and knowledgeable with the rest of the world, except when it is on their own terms, meaning the former British Empire. The fear of infection by foreigners still rings true in England's foreign relations today, while England believes itself incapable of any such malign influence on the outside world, like a previous outbreak of BSE (Mad Cow Disease) which infected English beef for export. And war has always loomed large in the life of this essentially martial, island race, so much so that one view of England surely is that of a war camp, always ready to send its armed forces to foreign posts to build upon England's historical military glory. As Shakespeare suggested then, and it is still true today, England is a monarchy, first and foremost, well suited for the interests of the ruling class and the military machine it continues to control and dominate. And who are "this happy breed of men" John of Gaunt mentions? Surely, the chosen few

---

[97] Ibid., Act II, Scene i, 11, 40–50.

men just like himself, like the Duke of Lancaster! From the pen of two modern-day historians comes the similar conclusion about their country: "England remains a monarchy, and—we insist—not merely cosmetically so. English sovereigns long ago lost significant personal power, but monarchic forms remain central not only to the legitimacy but also to the machinery of English state power… Royalty… epitomises a claim to legitimacy based…on antiquity, tradition, continuity, a self-conscious and carefully constructed *Englishness*. It is an emblem of what is held to set 'us' apart from other countries, with their 'parvenu' monarchs or their vulgarly elected heads of state."[98] No wonder the English still feel most comfortable in heralding the works of Shakespeare and pointing the rest of the world to him. After all these years, he still has the final word to say on England.

In modern times, since the eighteenth-century targets of English xenophobia has included particularly France, Germany, and the United States. All three countries have presented a threat to their control over the English people in one form or another—political, social, and cultural. As long as England could hold its head high among the nations as the mother country of a great empire, there was nothing really to fear from outside. However, with the waning of economic dominance in the late nineteenth century, and of political dominance in the early twentieth century, the fear of being surpassed and proven wrong fueled the tongues and pens of the Establishment's hacks to attack these particular countries who appeared to dominate world affairs, culturally and politically. It is not uncommon today to hear a very ordinary Englishman say, seemingly out of the blue, "The one people I really don't like is the French. And my family agrees with me." Such words of animosity, despite the Concorde and Channel Tunnel cooperative projects between the two countries in very recent times, not to mention the Atlantic Alliance, NATO, and the European Union, shock the outsider.

All three countries receiving the most severe xenophobic attacks from the English are republics with economies stronger than

---

[98] Corrigan, P. and Sayer, D., *The Great Arch: English State Formation as Cultural Revolution*, London, 1985, pp. 188–9.

England's, and with better educated and trained general populaces. It is difficult not to conclude that sheer envy and jealousy accounts for this externally directed loathing. "On the psychiatrists couch" England and the English would not render a very positive diagnosis for a healthy personality. Rather, an individual who is constantly criticizing others, as the English nation is doing to the rest of the world, often reveals someone who is insecure and unhappy with his own life and accomplishments. A healthy personality, in contrast, looks upon the world outside in a very positive, constructive light, as all part of one's own world, with its hopes and dreams. Some have seen England's failure in the twentieth century as one of faith in itself and nerve. Coupled with this failure is the unwillingness to go inside and do some serious soul-searching because the Establishment continues to tell the English people that England is best, and they find it easier to believe this than to change their institutions, too historic and revered in the English eyes, to tamper with. Meanwhile, the masses of English people sublimate their unhappiness as they have been taught to do. "Americans are always in a hurry and I'll confess I sometimes get aggravated by the slower tempo on crowded English sidewalks, especially if rushing for the Underground. But the speed, anger, and aggression you can sometimes get from British drivers and the occasional viciousness in speech and body language represents a kind of civility, a sheer meanness, I've seen nowhere else. It makes you wonder how much anxiety and alienation there is."[99]

Americans who are lifelong Anglophiles find such English behavior, especially when it is directed toward them, hurtful and shocking, contrary to their favorite image of the English Gentleman. Unless one adopts an English accent, English manners and clothing, acquires an English wife, and praises English genius, as did T. S. Eliot in his time—so the English can claim him as their own, which is what they did—the American always finds himself an alien in what he may regard as his mother country. "It is a very inhibiting thing to live in a country where you always are an alien. You won't meet any American here who has become English or who has any chance of becoming

---

[99] Critchfield, p. 462.

English. You can't do it... I mean probably the most pathetic sight here is an Anglophile who believes that he's rubbing along with the English and being treated as an equal by the English."[100]

Anti-Americanism is second nature to most of the English people. They learn it from an early age and continue on through with it all their lives. Bullying is a standard English practice amongst Establishment figures, learned in the public schools amongst their peers, and used effectively against challenges to their hegemony of power in later life. In an interview with the author, peer, and Establishment figure, Jeffrey Archer, the American Richard Critchfield wrote as follows,

> The ingratiating thing about Jeffrey Archer is just when you decide he's really pugnacious and awful, his face lights up with an impish grin and he says, 'I'm teasing, I'm teasing. You mustn't take me seriously.' And you realise that here is Jack the Giant Killer, Jorrocks riding to the hounds, still a Hardy boy who whooshes to the Pierre and Willard [New York hotels] by Concorde, plots how Americans and Russians almost blew each other up, and does it all with enormous zest... And what about the sixteen year old school-leavers unskilled and out of work? 'No one knows better than Americans that the great secret is to travel if you can't get what you want in your area'. English people don't like to move. 'Well, they should jolly well start'. Why aren't the English better entrepreneurs? 'We're a country with a thousand years' history. America's only just begun, Wild West cowboys making good'. *Okay, pard, time for a shoot-up.* Compare a supermarket here to one in America. Here the checkout girls [and boys] sit, there they stand. Here they just

---

[100] Paul Theroux, American author, Critchfield, p. 250.

shove your groceries aside, there they put them in a bag for you.

Archer bristled, satisfyingly provoked.

> Our goods are still as well made as anything America makes. We still work as hard. So let's don't imagine Americans work any harder. Let's don't imagine they are any better. My dealings with Americans, I've found them no better than we are'. In terms of? 'Energy, determination, ability, brains, history—anything you can name, we can beat the Americans [and the Germans too?].

Richard Critchfield then wrote in his own notes for himself, *Smile When You Say That...*

> That sounds like anti-Americanism. 'Of course not. I'm a great admirer of Americans. Just because I don't think they are as good as we are [except we sometimes do need their dollars and military might], doesn't mean I'm anti them. There's no connection at all'. I think Americans would bridle to hear you say that. 'If they bridle, it shows what very weak intellect they have'. What do Americans do, when you say you're better. 'I didn't say we were better,' Archer interrupted. 'I said we can do as well as they do. Please don't misquote me. As well as, any time'. That's why I need the tape recorder. So I don't misquote.[101]

Lord Archer later was charged with perjury and perverting the course of justice in a libel case from 1987 whereby he was imprisoned from 2001–2003.

---

[101] Critchfield, pp. 286–7.

Americans up and down England, whether in the time of Mark Twain, Consuelo Vanderbilt, or today, Richard Critchfield, can have similar kinds of jockeying, jerky, logically distorted conversations with ordinary English people: on the street, in classrooms, in universities, in churches, or at lunch, dinner, and drinks parties. The threat of America looms so great in the English psyche—with Germany a close second, and France not far behind—that anything goes as long as English pride and supremacy can be defended and upheld. What England once offered to the world under the Pax Britannia, all orchestrated carefully by the Establishment, was its subjection to a small elite who wished to enjoy themselves at the expense of mostly dark-skinned peoples around the world. Its Empire seemed enlightened to some people, even to some Americans, but the very word *empire* means conquer and rule, however compassionately some may perceive that rule to be. Freedom, personal freedom and liberty, for the earth's inhabitants under English political, economic, and cultural influence, was never part of the set-up; rather, the right to rule others was seen as a God-given privilege, granted to the English as *a chosen people.*

The idea and belief of English election dated back to the reign of Elizabeth I. "The Anglican Church seemed the living embodiment of England as the elect nation, the defeat of the Armada being the ultimate sign of God's favour."[102] Only two hundred years later, with England's defeat by the Americans in 1781, would this notion of election be shaken, but then blissfully ignored or sublimated. The final capping to England's election, to the English mind, came with the Establishment of a vast worldwide Empire. In 1897, at the great celebrations in England of Queen Victoria's sixtieth anniversary celebration of her accession to the throne, "Britain stood alone among the powers...[in] isolated splendour...[which] was specifically the product of Empire. Empire was the fount of pride. Empire was the panacea. *Empire was God's gift to the British race, and dominion was their destiny.*"[103]

---

[102] Corrigan and Sayer, p. 59.
[103] Morris, James [now Jan], *Heaven's Command: An Imperial Progress*, London, 1973, pp. 535–7.

Another nation which once had a mighty empire too, in fact the one the English Establishment always modelled its own upon, is Italy. One Italian took note of some salient English traits, especially apparent during their days of Empire. He wrote, "The black suit was merely a symbol, a tacit admission of British supremacy in almost all fields, with the exception of abstract philosophy, music, cuisine, and love-making, the admiration and envy for their wealth, power, sagacity, and *brutal ruthlessness*, whenever necessary."[104] This writer commented that many Continentals believed, as did the English, that they "could prolong the *status quo* indefinitely, and that there was nothing to worry about."[105]

History shows that this English *status quo* became unstuck because the world and its people were not static. Change comes, whether people like it or not. Some call this change progress; others simply long for the good old days before the changes inevitably appeared. To try to keep the world in check, at its command, the English developed a rather awesome secret service with agents all over the world. "The diabolical British Intelligence Service, which infiltrated its agents unnoticed everywhere and ferreted out the world's most jealously kept secrets, was particularly admired and feared."[106]

While the English have received their comeuppance through the events and realities of the twentieth century, they still cling onto a belief that they will be vindicated in the end, that awful America, Germany, and France will be driven back, somehow, into their rightful places under England's imperial dominion. "In a way, Britain still sees itself as the sceptered isle, cut from the Continent by divine will. If God had wanted to tie it to the rest of Europe, He would evidently not have dug the Channel."[107]

And what then of the European Union and England's place in it? Historically, the English called the Continentals disparaging names like "frog" and "kraut." "All these prejudices used to be expressed

---

[104] Barzini, Luigi, *The Europeans*, London, 1983, p. 37.
[105] Ibid., p. 41.
[106] Ibid., p. 43.
[107] Ibid., p. 59.

openly. Now they are politely kept hidden or lightly alluded to."[108] The Establishment is in favor of anything on earth as long as it can be in charge and in control. The English ethic in foreign relations, as in everything else in English life and institutions, is to bow to expediency in the interests of England's ruling class. Unfortunately, Europe today may pass the English by. "The English thought there was always time to catch [the European bus]. They were imperturbable by nature and tradition but also because they did not believe Europe was their business."[109]

As typical of the Englishman's contradictory nature, while he remains stoutly anti-American—opposing all things American as inferior to English, including the American people themselves—England publicly proclaims "a special relationship" with the United States and supports American foreign policy, mostly as consistent with English interests abroad. Since the nation can no longer achieve glory by its own foreign relations, England rides unashamedly on America's coattails as the world's only super power, while receiving the world's only superpower's unwitting protection from the full scorn and wrath of its European neighbors for continually blocking or impeding the councils and decisions of the EU. In fact, it had no choice but to abandon its world role after the Suez Crisis in 1956— "the turning-point that shocked Britain into the modem world," or so says the English press today, perhaps a bit prematurely.[110] Not out of character for the English Establishment, "Eden lied over Suez" as revealed by the press recently.[111] Whether the English Prime Minister lied in Parliament or not in late 1956 was always irrelevant to President Eisenhower, who would not support the cooked-up deal between England, France, and Israel to keep the Suez Canal under British control. "The threat that Nasser's [president of Egypt] pan-Arabism posed to Western interests was outweighed by America's deep strain of anti-imperialism. Without America the game was up. What was the legacy of Suez? The illusion of global power was shat-

---

[108] Ibid., p. 59.
[109] Ibid., p. 64.
[110] "Forty Years On," editorial in *Times*, July 29, 1996, p. 19.
[111] "Secret Accord Shows Eden Lied Over Suez," *Times*, October 17, 1996, p. 11.

tered, and British prestige in the Middle East never recovered... In the Falklands, in Ulster, and then in the Gulf and Bosnia, Britain was to recover its pride in its thoroughly professional armed forces...but after Suez it is hard for us ever being triumphalist again."[112]

Sadly, the island mentality of the English people and Establishment prevents it from properly seeing and. therefore, understanding any viewpoint about life and the world, except England's own. It confuses England's historic interests and ambitions with America's, and even Germany's. The English love of war is not really a part of American and German life, where the emphasis for human fulfilment is on personal creativity and, many times, for the glory of God. England sees glory to this day as something it alone should have and deserve. In the past, and probably in the future, this glory would be achieved at the expense of other people's liberty.

In effect, the English mind has a very superficial, immature, and adolescent dream of "if I ruled the world." Pax Americana is not about domination through imperialism, as some would like to believe, whether economic, cultural, or political. Rather, the American peace is based on an historic mission to spread the ideas of the Declaration of Independence of 1776 to the peoples of the earth. Individual Americans may sometimes be seen to be failing to fulfil this mission by their activities based upon greed and personal power. An American correspondent of the *Sunday Times* for four decades wrote thus, "No doubt, the idea of a Pax Americana goes against the American grain."

Nonetheless, American influence has spread and continues to spread rapidly throughout the world because "it promoted the idea of freedom of the individual and improved living standards through economic growth." In contrast was Pax Britannica: "The Pax Americana does not imply, as it did the Pax Britannica, formal control over a great number of countries around the globe or easy access to raw materials or great international advantages—not even the satisfaction of being able to exert a civilizing influence." [113]

---

[112] "Forty Years On," *Times*, p. 19.
[113] Henry Brandon, Critchfield, p. 287.

Under America's worldwide influence in the world since 1945 and today, barring no other nations, the peoples of the earth are offered a possibility for personal freedom and development unlike any time in mankind's history. The English refuse to understand the implications of personal freedom, perhaps being terrified of it them-selves after centuries of central control by an elite. Therefore, the English prefer to look upon the American Republic as a mere blip in world history, an irregularity which will soon go away. Patience and the willingness to wait their time is all that is needed. Therefore, they studiously refuse to learn about how the American government func-tions, whether on a federal, state, or local level. They refuse to learn American history, except as it flatters and reflects their own history, while hopefully detracting from the 244-year American success story. Such details regarding the American Revolution, which may have no historic basis are cleverly expounded in English secondary school textbooks today, "There were cases where Americans skinned Indians to use them for leather."[114] Such inflammatory undocumented state-ments only conjure up visions of Nazi practices during the 1940s. Is this the English intention to equate the American Revolution with the atrocities of Hitler's Third Reich? In earlier English textbooks, the general tone was subjective throughout: "The [Revolutionary] War [was] often barely mentioned, or the Americans shown to be a backward…people, no match for British regulars, but helped to vic-tory by Britain's European enemies."[115] No wonder England creates and embraces people the likes of Jeffrey Archer!

Being from an imperturbable people the English Establishment never gives up, never admits defeat, or never confesses its cruelties and barbarisms against human beings over the centuries. Its gift to the world is always itself. Meanwhile, the Germans have rebuilt their war-torn country in the past 75 years to become Europe's major economic power. The United States persevered over the totalitarianism of the USSR to emerge victorious after fifty years of Cold War. The English

---

[114] Evans, R. E., *The War of American Independence*, Cambridge University Press, 1976, p. 43.
[115] Ibid., p. 43.

continue to grumble at both these very successful nations, instead of licking their own wounds from their economic and moral decline in the league of nations, and venturing forth into a brave new world, this time in concert with its European partners, rather than as the aloof island fortress it has chosen to be historically. Instead, over the past 75 years, it has continued to relive its "finest hour," as if that was the shed-water point in the history of the human race.

It would be to the world's relief if the English would stop badgering and criticizing all the other nations that have surpassed it and, instead, solve its own problems and make those painful and necessary changes in its institutions to give greater freedom and self-respect to its own people. Sadly, many of the English act like immigrants in their own country, where forelock pulling has always been the form. A recent letter in an American newspaper regarding the Englishman Peter Mayle, whose books on Provence have made him very rich, was headlined, "Sour Grapes?" It is a representative letter because it can so easily apply to the English nation, as the rest of the world continues to see it, through its daily comments and actions toward the rest of us.

> How ironic that Mr Mayle now writes patronizingly about the Hamptons [Long Island, USA] as he once did about Provence. Not only ironic, but the height of ingratitude as well—since it is only after he made his money writing about the South of France and its people that he can now afford to live in the Hamptons. I would remind Mr Mayle of this Arab proverb: 'Never spit in the well as you pass by, for you never know when you'll have to drink from it again.' Unless of course, like him, you were made persona-non-grata in the beautiful well that is known as Provence.[116]

And so to England, stop spitting in our wells!

---

[116] P. Camps, Saillon, France, *International Herald Tribune*, September 10, 1996, p. 1.

CHAPTER X

Ethics in the Church of England:
God Is an Englishman

The reign of King Henry VIII in the mid-sixteenth century saw the triumphant fusion of church and state, a political and ecclesiastical Anschluss. The Tudor king, unhappy with the state of his own personal life as well as the finances of his realm, made an abrupt U-turn, away from being a favored son of the papacy to one of its most rebellious and odious. No longer the "Defender of the Faith" in the eyes of Pope Leo X, who had given Henry this honored title in 1521 for opposing the activities of the peasant priest, Martin Luther in Germany, whom Henry dubbed that "scabby and incurable sheep." While all his life the king remained outwardly a religious man, having devoted many early years of his life to the study of theology, he succeeded in pushing the pope out of England. This revolt against Rome was done to secure the king's own happiness by marrying Anne Boleyn after first divorcing Catherine of Aragon. One historian has noted the following regarding this extraordinary split in the Christian Church, "Nothing in the long history of the separation of the Church of England from the Church of Rome is more astonishing than that the King encountered so little opposition to his plans."[117] Such noteworthy opposition coming from the likes of John

---

[117] Neil, Stephen, *Anglicanism*, 4th edition, New York, 1978, p. 41.

Fisher, Bishop of Rochester, and Thomas More, once lord chancellor, were dealt a blow to the neck by the king, as were two of his six wives. There is no doubt that this Tudor Monarch, who succeeded in bringing the English state to a smoothly running, absolutist form "was a resolute and dangerous person."[118] No one dared to oppose him, including family, in his lifetime.

This centralization of the state in England, unknown in any country up until then since the Romans declared Caesar to be a god, ensured the consolidation of totalitarianism in English institutions, all under the name of "the Crown in Parliament." The "nationalization...of the Church—the decisive shift from being the Church in England...to the Church of England, under the supremacy of the Crown—was...'undoubtedly the greatest single augmentation of which royal authority has ever received.'"[119] Great wealth accrued to the Crown with its seizure of monastic properties. Royal supremacy was ensured when the Crown seized the churches as its own because they contained "at the time the most extensive apparatus of propaganda, the pulpit, and moral regulation, the Church Courts, in the land."[120] The medieval balance of power between church and state was shifted in favor of the state for the first time in Christendom. "'The breach with Rome brought out the unmedieval idea that the king was supreme in every sphere of life, and that England was a self-sufficient empire, with Henry as its emperor, subject to no other authority on earth. Henceforth, the king would be addressed... as 'Your Majesty', a unique being exalted above all others in both Church and State.'"[121] Officially sanctioned and ingrained propaganda of the 1530s contained the seeds of the notion of England as an elect nation, while Englishmen themselves became increasingly aware "of the intrusive presence of the central government."[122]

The notorious Act of Supremacy, 1534, recognized royal headship of the church and gave the Crown the power to conduct visi-

---

[118] Ibid., p. 43.
[119] Corrigan and Sayers, p. 45.
[120] Ibid., p. 46.
[121] Ibid., p. 47.
[122] Ibid., pp. 47–8.

tations on the clergy. "Henry's theological knowledge and self-righteousness gave his supremacy a dangerously personal character, and it is well for the future health of the national church that his immediate successors were a minor and two women, all less inclined and less able to undertake the personal services of caesaropapalism."[123] In succeeding reigns, the supremacy of the Monarch in church affairs was softened somewhat by designating the Monarch "Supreme Governor of the Church of England," which Elizabeth II is still called today.

The question needs to be raised as to whether the English people, as a whole, have an innate spiritual inclination beyond the paganism of their Anglo-Saxon forebears. Are they rather accustomed, as were the Anglo-Saxons, to having their religion imposed upon them from the top down? The social and class structure, on the other hand, has always seemed to be second nature to the English. It is more tangible, less introspective to translate all of human relationship between men and toward the deity in social arrangements. A hierarchical sense of society, in which every individual knows their place, gives the English some kind of earthly security, apparently, while higher thoughts of metaphysics make them uneasy and even baffle them. Hence, the English have always been light on the ground in producing philosophers, theologians, and musical composers as compared to the extent and profundity of the contributions made in these areas by their first cousins, the Germans. A pleasure-seeking and materialistic society based upon the myriad of forms derived from social class, such as is apparent in a Jane Austen novel, is really the Englishman's cup of tea.

Why there was so little opposition to Henry VIII's revolutionary policies in the 1530s and 1540s can be most easily explained by these very English characteristics. A military society lends itself quite easily to this mode of life, alternating between heroic battles and grand conquests, and resting in camp with the pleasures of parties, dances, games, and pantomimes. Such was the life in the great English country houses before September 1939. The church remained an important prop in this military-social class Establishment, as the central

---

[123] Dickens, A. G., *The English Reformation*, 4th printing, New York, 1974, pp. 119–20.

state's important means of maintaining public order, of keeping the masses of people under control. But as the gateway to heaven for eternal life, the Englishman probably could care less. Surely since Henrician times in the sixteenth century, and up to the present, king and country come before God in the hierarchy of an Englishman's loyalties. While the Americans have placed boldly on all their coins and paper money, "In God We Trust," the English have placed the monarch's face or profile, along with "R G Reg F D" on all coins, signifying that the Monarch is "Defender of the Faith" and "By the Grace of God." Ostensibly, it is the Christian faith being defended, but it was a title given to one man, Henry VIII, by the Pope in 1521 for defending Christianity against Martin Luther's teachings. By 1533, the English Monarch had been excommunicated by the next Pope so the Church of England would be in schism with Rome ever afterwards. God gets short shrift in the English honor system. In order of precedent in the realm of England, the archbishop of Canterbury comes second after the Monarch. The English argument is that while the Church of England is an established or official church in the land, it is not state controlled. Hence, its pulpits are perfectly free for the airing of all kinds of political controversy, except as a criticism of the Monarch, who is the hereditary head of state. Prayers in the official Book of Common Prayer of the Church of England are read out for the Monarch and other members of the Royal Family. Bishops and deans in the church are appointed by the Prime Minister with the approval of the Monarch. Someone who regularly denounces, or even occasionally criticizes the Royal Family would not receive one of these top church appointments.

The clergy of the Church of England may give the appearance of openness to the movement of the Holy Spirit in their sermons and teachings, but centuries of central state control over the Church of England inform them instinctively where the line must be drawn as not to offend the Establishment over which the Monarch still reigns, or worse yet, to lose their careers and heads.

How church and politics do mix in the highest levels of English ecclesiastical life is evident by public statements made by successive archbishops of Canterbury, supporting the military actions and wars of the country. Not to do so would be considered treason by many, as when George Bell, Bishop of Chichester, tried to persuade the House of Lords and the nation to stop the extensive civilian bombing of Nazi Germany and to make a distinction amongst the German people of Nazis and their opponents. He also advocated making peace and stopping the war through contact with the German Resistance Movement, which sought the overthrow of Hitler and his Nazi followers. Although well-suited for the job, he never was called to be Archbishop of Canterbury, ostensibly because he reminded the conscience of his nation that two wrongs do not make a right.

A more recent newspaper revelation shows that in the 1960s, when Michael Ramsey was Archbishop of Canterbury, he was "encouraged" by Harold Wilson, then Prime Minister, to publicly support the use of "force against the UDI supporters in Rhodesia, even though he knew his Cabinet had already decided against it." When the speech was made by the Archbishop, "media-led thunderclaps erupted over Lambeth Palace and Ramsey was lacerated in political circles. There was little in the way of support from Wilson's Downing Street."[124] Similarly, the morning the Gulf War began in 1991, the then Archbishop of Canterbury, Robert Runcie, was on Radio 4's popular *Today* program, telling his Establishment audience why the war was "just."

In a recent furor in the press over the publication of a former Archbishop of Canterbury's biography, *The Reluctant Archbishop* by Humphrey Carpenter, himself the son of a former Bishop of Oxford, various remarks by Robert Runcie were said to his biographer in private, which then appeared in the book, including negative asides about members of the Royal Family. Runcie was made very uncomfortable by the publication of his "off-the-record" remarks. All this fuss generated many different kinds of articles in print, including talk of the Prince of Wales' fitness to be king as a confessed adulterer who is seen by the man who married him in 1981 as someone who should "love the Church of England a bit more." Such words strike a new chord with people who regard the future king as Defender

---

[124] "Wilson's Secret," *Times*, April 9, 1996, p. 14.

of the Faith and Supreme Governor of the Church of England. To make matters worse, Runcie was then quoted as saying, "But I think he'd given up on the Church of England before I arrived."[125] Was the marriage between the Prince and Princess of Wales arranged? Runcie thought it was, but then, too, he said, "For the Royal Family, survival is the priority." An heir to the throne was needed to keep the House of Windsor going. Again, who comes first—the English Monarch or God?

A Roman Catholic religious columnist in the English press, well-known, pondered the Runcie biography furor in one of his columns. He took into account the former Archbishop's sense of betrayal by his biographer for printing his remarks, recorded on a tape machine, which Runcie had hoped would be more selectively edited before the publication of his story. He wrote,

> The rules in question were gleaned from *the code of honour of a Gentleman*—public school, officer's mess, the Athenaeum, whatever. One of the key principles in this code is that private remarks stay private... As the Archbishop of Canterbury he saw "being a Gentleman" and "loving the Church of England", as two sides of the same coin; it was simply that he had no space in his philosophy for non-Anglicans (or non-gentlemen), people who did not play by his rules. Not being an Anglican was somehow disreputable. I am sure he regards Prince Charles' alleged lack of enthusiasm for the Church of England as something to be ashamed of.[126]

The writer then pointed out to his readers just what the Church of England looks like to someone such as himself, where true religion

---

[125] "I think Charles Had Already Given Up On The Church," *Times*, September 9, 1996, p. 16.

[126] "The Tribulations of One of the Church's Perfect Gentlemen," by Clifford Longley, *Daily Telegraph*, September 13, 1996, p. 27.

is concerned with the centrality of the mass, rather than the honor of a Gentleman trying to be Archbishop of Canterbury.

> It seemed to me Robert Runcie was in love with a certain idea of Christian England, in which all the honourable Christian virtues were combined...a subtle and sublime England of good manners, green grass and *mild religion*. He always reminded me of a certain sort of decent country solicitor, safe as houses, shrewd as a poet, a fine church warden but no more holy than the next man. For such people, religion is much more about being polite to God than about scaling the heights of mysticism.[127]

Such a concept of God is surely not a new creation but the product of a church, severely subjected to the state after five hundred years of a Babylonian captivity. Young people, such as the Prince of Wales once was, find no real substance in a religion braced by strict rules, moral and social, while lacking a real upwardly divine center. Polite society has very little to do with Calvary and salvation. The English religion, like everything else in English life, has been socialized, so the English can identify with it and enjoy it. Christianity, as it was known in England prior to the Reformation, was mystical and otherworldly in its most important aspects through the Sacraments. English mystics were not unknown in the Church, such as Austin Baker. The Reformation succeeded in making it pedestrian and subject to the Crown, just another English club and a branch of the state.

The cry today heard from the supporters of the Church of England, particularly the clergy, is that the secular world is impinging upon the teaching of the Church, causing people to abandon it for New-Age religion, horoscopes, and the occult, generally. A recent report showed that English people held numerous beliefs inconsistent with the Christian faith. As the established Church of England for five

---

[127] Ibid., p. 27.

centuries now, the main responsibility for this decline in Christian practice has to be placed on the state religion. "Even practising Christians held unorthodox, New Age-style beliefs, further evidence that society was in danger of losing touch with its Judaeo-Christian roots, according to the report on the 'Search for Faith'. While most people still had spiritual beliefs, Britain was witnessing the upsurge of a form of 'folk religion', epitomised by Mystic Meg and horoscopes."[128]

The term *spiritual beliefs* is really quite meaningless in terms of the Christian religion, where the church has always recognized that the world is filled with many kinds of spirits, but there can only be one true spirit out of them all—the Holy Spirit, who alone leads people to Christ, and therefore, Salvation (Romans 8 and 1 John 4:1–6).

That some people in the Church of England do recognize there are evil spirits was evident in the ongoing feud at Lincoln Cathedral, where the dean and sub-dean argued mightily together starting about 1990. Neither man would leave the cathedral, despite being asked to do so by the Bishop of Lincoln and the Archbishop of Canterbury. The Dean of Lincoln declared that the cathedral should be exorcised, and everyone from the bishop down be sacked.[129]

Elsewhere, the evil presences are not unknown in the Church of England, these days at least. When the famous "9 o'clock service" in a Church of England parish in Sheffield was discovered to be a medium for less than Christian activity, church leaders who previously supported the vicar, Chris Brain, reacted in horror, while washing their hands of any responsibility in the matter. Damaged lives, particularly those of women, were revealed through abusive sexual and psychological practices by the vicar himself, a kind of guru to the people searching for a spiritual meaning in their lives. Instead of leading them to Christ, Brain led them to himself, making himself the center point of their religion.

Many of Brain's congregation considered
him a prophet sent to save the western world by

---

[128] "Faith in Horoscopes a Sign of Moral Decay, Says Churches," by Ruth Gledhill, *Times*, November 11, 1996, p. 5.

[129] "Shut the Cathedral, Says Dean in Feud," *Times*, November 11, 1996, p. 5.

reinventing Christianity for the twenty-first century [just as Henry VIII did for the Church of England in the sixteenth century]. Yet his teachings were distinctively unorthodox. He encouraged his "inner circle" to be unfaithful to their spouses and to raise "spiritual energy" by masturbating, and offered women healing through an exploration of sexual intimacy with him. Brain, who left school with only a handful of O-levels, was a genius at manipulating and exploiting his congregation while at the same time duping theologians, academics and the Anglican authorities.[130]

A church centered upon Christ and his teachings in the New Testament, would less likely have overlooked and put up with such a phenomena so obviously wicked. It is apparent that the gentlemen of the Anglican Church were no match for the spiritual adventures of Chris Brain. Until it was pointed out to them otherwise by victims of the evil vicar, the Anglican gentlemen of the Church of England seemed to have enjoyed watching Brain's show.

The discussion continues today in England, as in the recent past, whether the Church of England should be disestablished and, once again, become the Church *in* England. It is one of those discussions the Establishment enjoys having aired because it gives others the impression of society's openness and freedom, a willingness to look at its faults, and even correct them. Like all similar discussions in public about the Crown, the Parliament, the judiciary, the class system, the educational system—nothing ever really changes as a result of it. The status quo is finally preserved, probably to the relief of all.

One brave newspaper editor, however, declared that enough is enough.

That Establishment has had its day. Disestablishment would not only be a kind of con-

---

[130] "The Raving Reverend," Roland Howard, *Sunday Times*, August 25, 1996, p. 28.

stitutional purgative, removing one of the many shams that litter the forecourts of Westminster. It would be healthier for the Church as a spiritual formation: the ministry of its priests and curates does not need government, its bishops do not need their House of Lords seats. Where is the contemporary John Wesley to see that the revival of the Church's spiritual mission requires its emancipation from the fetid and gossip-friendly connection with the state?[131]

Not just the church, but every institution of English life needs a similar emancipation from the state. As long as the men of the Establishment go unchallenged, however, the system will perpetuate itself, as it has for centuries. Each new Archbishop of Canterbury will be just like all the others since the Reformation, where Monarch and country are just ahead of Jesus the Christ, who is not English.

Sadly, the number of the Church of England's communicants diminishes with each passing year. The death knell is sounding for the Established Church as no more than 5 percent of the English people attend its services each week, a number surpassed by the once renegade and disgraced Roman Catholic Church in England. In the United States, where the church is disestablished by virtue of its written constitution, 40 percent of the American people attend church regularly each week, in a county where the largest, single, religious denomination is Roman Catholic.

The sister church of the Church of England in America, the Episcopal Church, has dropped in membership since the 1950s from 2.2 percent of the population to 0.85 percent of the American people today. The Reformation succeeded in lopping off the branch of the Anglican Church from the main body of Christianity. After five hundred years, the Church of England may be finally withering away and dying.

---

[131] "Antidisestablishmentarianism Confounded," *Independent*, September 11, 1996, p. 13.

EPILOGUE

The English Ethic Unbared

The English ethic, based upon the cult of the Gentleman, created and maintained by the Establishment as a device to maintain political and social power over the English people, came into force following the centralization of the English state under Henry VIII, though not immediately. The previous Christian ethic remained in place for a while. But it was always reluctantly accepted by the English people whose untranscendent nature made them a bit squeamish and uncomfortable with a system of conduct based upon the intangible otherness of God in Christ. The English Gentleman evolved, from the days of chivalry into the embodiment of the English ethical ideal. No country in the Christian world took the Gentleman so seriously or ascribed to it so much ethical importance as did the English. Not only did it satisfy the English longing to socialize every aspect of life, including religion, but also it satisfied the English habit of compromise, believing in the end that everyone could be kept happy under the elitist rule of such men.

The English removed the responsibility of the individual for personal morality long ago by placing it upon the social group as a whole. Anyone could act like a Gentleman, if he learned the correct form, which meant he had to go through the right educational process, which alone taught that form. Those who did not learn the correct form would be shepherded through life by the English Gentleman, who retained control of the social and political and religious structures. The Gentleman became a code of behavior, requiring no soul-searching, no introspection on the part of the individual. Rather, it was either correct form or not, according to a rule book (albeit an unwritten one), a favorite Establishment practice so that the oral tradition safeguarded the secret to power among the upper class—sacred words only spoken within its ranks and incomprehensible to those below and to outsiders.

The moral individualism practiced in America, where each citizen, each individual American, is regarded as a moral being, responsible for his own actions is unknown in England. "As political theorist James Rutherford notes: 'The free and equal individual with moral responsibility is the basis of communal solidarity'... That community in democratic pluralistic America is grounded in the individual as a thinking, moral actor, not in group solidarity."[132]

The English, today especially, wish to compare themselves to the Americans in every way imaginable, for better or for worse. Yet their ethic prevents them from seeing how ludicrous such comparisons are—rather like comparing a watermelon to a grape, a very English sour grape at that! They remain blind to the very real social, cultural, and political differences that have divided the American Republic from the English Absolutist State for over two centuries.

Due to their ethic, mostly, the English remain elusive to the rest of the world, except to those countries whose history and political structures are similar to England's. That remarkable team of filmmakers who have attempted to capture Edwardian England for moviegoers in America and elsewhere, James Ivory, Ismail Merchant, and Ruth Jhabvala, speak so typically of outsiders who wish England and the English only the very best, but remain puzzled by English behavior.

James Ivory, born in America, wrote, "I felt at home in England. I felt a rapport with the people. At the same time I always thought the English said to themselves—about me—'Oh, such a nice American, not like the others at all!'"

Ruth Jhabvala, born in Germany and relocated in England as a teenager during the 1930s, "never said anything bad about the

---

[132] Lipset, S., p. 275.

English. Other than when doors were slammed in our faces, and she would say, 'You must expect that. That's the way they are.'"[133] While no longer living in England, Ruth commented further, "'My feeling for England will always be of profound gratitude. I wouldn't be alive if it weren't for England... Were doors slammed in my face? No, not really. But then, I didn't attempt to open any, maybe that's why not. I was, you might say, a bit on the edge.'"[134]

An English friend who knew Ruth in the 1950s in India wrote of her attitude to England and English customs as follows, "'I cannot remember her speaking of England at all, the country or the place or anything to do with it, but she was always intrigued by 'Englishness' in a slightly ironic way. She would say, 'Ohh so strong, so fine, so tall—how wonderful to be like you... She'd appear to admire all that, but with a sweet edge of mockery, though mockery is too kind a word.'"[135]

Since English hypocrisy is a subject in some of the Merchant-Ivory films, James Ivory commented on a Cambridge University official who tried to thwart the filming of *Maurice*, where "hypocrites lie as thick upon the ground...as autumn leaves." He said, "'This man had a pale face with lanky hair over a skull-like brow. And as Ismail took him to one side, I really thought he was not human. This was the kind of man who voted for the execution of Charles I... *maddened and inflexible, and very English.*'"[136] Cambridge remains one of the bastions of the English Establishment, where the English Gentlemen are produced en masse.

The final result of all this inflexible English madness is that the country is slowly being suffocated to death. Much to the Englishman's chagrin, outsiders find it to be a place where nothing is going on, except what the English are saying to one another, doing to one another, while shouting out at the rest of us like a bitter old man. The subject of an earlier Merchant-Ivory film, the Indian Nirad

---

[133] Pym, John (foreword by James Ivory), *Merchant Ivory's English Landscape: Rooms. Views and Anglo-Saxon Attitudes*, New York, 1995, p. 23.
[134] Ibid., p. 24.
[135] Catherine Freeman, Pym, p. 105.
[136] Pym, p. 69.

C. Chandhuri, who wrote an autobiography of his life during the British Raj, also commented on England. "He observes that England is now a country where nothing happens, that if you open an English newspaper there's nothing in it... In England nothing's going on— and in a way I have to agree with him," said James Ivory. "I turn on the breakfast television in London, just as I do in New York, and what do I invariably get by way of 'news'? A lot of political backbiting, men haranguing in the House of Commons; dull stuff from the City; and of course sports."[137]

The friendly outsider would like to take the English aside and say to them, "Just what do you think you're doing! Why do you look upon much of the rest of the world as your adversary rather than as your partner in peace? Why do you refuse to throw your lot in with humanity instead of holding yourselves aloof, as if you are not really one of us at all?"

Someday, the English may be willing to listen to well-meaning advice. In the meantime, in England, among the English, business is as usual. Britannia still rules the waves, as if she ever truly did. The Land of Hope and Glory is the best place in the world, in English eyes, because God is an Englishman, and the English are his elect, chosen people. However, until God can be restored to His rightful place of glory, above Monarch and country as of old, England will continue on its prideful path of self-interest. England's friends in America and elsewhere can only stand by, helpless before a people who believe they always must be first and right, in a land, where even today "a man does things no Gentleman should do as only a Gentleman can." Here lies the English ethic unbared.

---

[137] Ibid., p. 27.

REFERENCES

Books and Essays

Annan, Noel. 1995. *Our Age* (paperback edition) London.

Barnett, Correlli. 1995. *The Lost Victory*. London.

Barzini, Luigi. 1983. *The Europeans*. London.

Bentley, Michael. 1984. *Politics without Democracy 1815–1914*. London.

Black, H. C. 1951. *Black's Law Dictionary* (4th edition). St. Paul, Minnesota.

Boothby, Lord. 1962. *My Yesterday, Your Tomorrow*. London.

Corrigan, Philip and Derek Sayer. 1985. *The Great Arch: English State Formation as Cultural Revolution*. London.

Critchfield, Richard. 1990. *Among the British: An Outsider's View*. London.

Cross, F. L. and B. A. Livingston (eds.). 1974. *Oxford Dictionary of the Christian Church*. London.

Danzinger, Danny (ed.). 1988. *Eton Voices*. London.

Dickens, A. G. 1974. *The English Reformation* (4th printing). New York.

Evans, R. E. 1976. *The War of American Independence*. Cambridge University Press.

Flew, Antony (ed. consultant). 1979. *A Dictionary of Philosophy*. London, p. 41.

Hennessy, Peter. 1990. "The Lion and the Unicorn Repolished." University of Reading, Department of Politics Occasional Paper No. 1: February.

Hollister, C. Warren. 1976. *The Making of England 55 BC–1399 AD*. Lexington, Massachusetts.

Hoare, Philip. 1990. *Serious Pleasures: The Life of Stephen Tennant*. London.

Hutton, Will. 1996. *The State We're In* (fully revised edition, first published 1988). London: Vintage.

Ivory, James, foreword to *Merchant Ivory's English Landscape: Rooms, Views and Anglo-Saxon Attitudes* by John Pym. New York, 1995.

Lees-Milne, James. 1984. *Another Self* (first published 1970). London.

Leeson, Nick, and Edward Whitley. 1996. *Rogue Trader*. London.

Lipset, Seymour Martin. 1996. *American Exceptionalism: A Double-Edged Sword*. New York.

Mason, Philip. 1982. *The English Gentleman: The Rise and Fall of an Ideal*. New York.

Morris, James (now Jan). 1973. *Heaven's Command: An Imperial Progress*. London.

Neil, Stephen. 1978. *Anglicanism* (4th edition). New York.

Robertson, David. 1986. *Dictionary of Politics*. London.

Shakespeare, William. 1956. *King Richard II* edited by Peter Ure (the Arden edition). London.

Tawney, R. H. 1926. *Religion and the Rise of Capitalism*. New York.

Trevelyan, G. M. 1953. *History of England* (first published in London in 1926). Vol. 1. Garden City: Anchor Books.

Wiener, Martin J. 1981. *English Culture and the Decline of the Industrial Spirit, 1850–1980*. Cambridge.

Magazines

Sam Willets. 1996. "A Bloody Good Game." *American Way* (American Airlines flight magazine), October 15, 1996.

"Who Cares Who We Are?" (editorial). *Country Life*, February 1, 1996.

John Russell. 1986. "Portrait of the British." *New York Times*, March 9, 1986.

Roland Howard. 1996. "The Raving Reverend." *Sunday Times*, August 25, 1996.

Newspapers

"Antidisestablishmentarianism Confounded." 1996. *Independent*, September 11, 1996.

Beeston, Richard. 1996. "Soviet Echo as Successor States Rule Awards Table." *Times*, August 5, 1996.

"Britain Must Resist the Court." 1996. *Times*, February 22, 1996.

"British Pass Broad Search Powers." 1996. *International Herald Tribune*, April 4, 1996.

Curphey, Marianne. 1995. "Royalty: Still a Draw?" *Times*, February 2, 1995.

Dionne, E. J. 1996. "Letter from P Camps, Saillon, France." *International Herald Tribune*, September 10, 1996.

"Euro 96: The Final Analysis." 1996. *Times*, July 1, 1996.

Eyres, Harry. 1996. "Three Cheers for Our Jolly Good Sports." *Daily Telegraph*, July 2, 1996.

Fenton, Ben and Robert Hardmen. 1996. "It's All Over for England." *Daily Telegraph*, June 27, 1996.

"Fools Gold" (editorial). 1996. *Times*, August 5, 1996.

"Forty Years On" (editorial). 1996. *Times*, July 29, 1996.

Gibb, Francis (legal correspondent). 1996. "Pressure Grows for Bill of Rights." *Times*, February 22, 1996.

Gledhill, Ruth. 1996. "Faith in Horoscopes a Sign of Moral Decay." *Times*, November 11, 1996.

Hughes, Rob. 1996. "The World Will Focus on this Ball." *International Herald Tribune*, June 8–9, 1996.

"I Think Charles Had Already Given Up on the Church." 1996. *Times*, September 9, 1996.

Letts, Quentin. 1996. "Greed Eclipses Olympic Creed of Atlanta 'Flea Market.'" *Times*, August 3, 1996.

Lewis, Anthony. 1996. "Constitutional Change in Britain?" *International Herald Tribune*, October 31, 1996.

_____. 1997. "Startling New Police Bill Meets Yawns in Britain." *International Herald Tribune*, December 31, 1996–January 1, 1997.

Lewis, Flora. 1996. "Britain Must Grow Up and Stop the Tantrums." *International Herald Tribune*, June 27, 1996

"Lloyds to Raise Offer to Names." 1996. *International Herald Tribune*, April 11, 1996.

Longley, Clifford. 1996. "The Tribulations of One of the Church's Perfect Gentlemen." *Daily Telegraph*, September 13, 1996.

Miller, David. 1996. "When Silver is as Good as Gold." *Times*, July 15, 1996.

Miller, David. 1996. "Redgrave Stands Supreme Among the Olympian Elite." *Times*, July 29,1996.

Mitchell, Kevin. 1996. "Raw Triumphalism and No Pure Horror." *Observer*, July 28, 1996.

O'Leary, John. 1996. "Public Schools Win More Places at Oxford." *Times*, August 26, 1996/

Parris, Matthew. 1995. "Straight Man Steals the Show." *Times*, November 30, 1995.

"Poor Man of Europe Lags Behind Continent." 1996. *Times*, June 27, 1996.

Powell, David. 1996. "Christie Mystery Comes to False End." *Times*, July 29, 1996.

Redwood, John. 1996. "Stand Up to Germany, On and Off the Field." *Times*, June 26, 1996.

Redwood, John and Linda Grant. 1996. "Under Pressure." *Guardian*, March 11, 1996.

Rees-Mogg, William. 1996. "Crown and Constitution." *Times*, August 1, 1996.

Scott, Brough. 1996. "Opening Gambit Strikes Gold in Memorable Style." *Sunday Telegraph*, July 21, 1996.

"Secret Accord Shows Eden Lied Over Suez." 1996. *Times*, October 17, 1996.

Shrimsley, Robert. 1996. "Major Pledges to Defend Freedoms." *Daily Telegraph*, June 27, 1996.

"Shut the Cathedral, Says Dean in Feud." 1996. *Times*, November 11, 1996.

"Thatcher Stuns Chinese Hosts by Predicting Political Change." 1996. *International Herald Tribune*, November 15, 1996.

Toynbee, Polly. 1996. "The Subtleties of Snobbery." *Independent*, June 26, 1996.

"UN Finds Separate Worlds of Rich and Poor Widening." 1996. *International Herald Tribune*, July 16, 1996.

"Wilson's Secret." 1996. *Times*, April 9, 1996.

Radio

Cooke, Alistair. 1996. *Letter from America*, Radio 4, January 21, 1996.

_____. 1996. *Letter from America*, Radio 4, March 17, 1996.

_____. 1996. *Letter from America*, Radio 4, April 21, 1996.

_____. 1996. *Letter from America*, Radio 4, May 5, 1996.

INDEX

CPSIA information can be obtained
at www.ICGtesting.com
Printed in the USA
FSHW011705110421
80264FS